Mothering in the late capitalist ruins can be, counterintuitively, extremely lonely work. Jennifer Case's brilliant essay collection not only describes how and why this is true but also remedies some of that resounding isolation. Case keeps company with her reader, offering the reparative gift of her attention and fine wordsmithing. Like Louise Erdrich and Anne Lamott, she turns the experience of early motherhood into literature.

— Elizabeth Rush, author of *The Quickening: Creation and Community at the Ends of the Earth*

A searing and beautiful portrait of motherhood in America. With propulsive prose and stunning detail, Jennifer Case chronicles not just the birth of her two children but also the transformation that women undergo as they learn to care for and love their children.

— Michaeleen Doucleff, author of *Hunt, Gather, Parent: What Ancient Cultures Can Teach Us about the Lost Art of Raising Happy, Helpful Little Humans*

Jennifer Case's lyrical, absorbing essay collection offers many kinds of birth stories. Yet her most piercing, revelatory attention is applied to the birth of the mother—this person who, while nursing, must learn to eat with a nondominant hand; this person whose safety and care are unjustly shaped by race and class; this person who navigates a new life that is so often fearful and lonely. Through it all, Case makes a wise, persistent case for community, collectivism, and hope.

— Belle Boggs, author of *The Art of Waiting: On Fertility, Medicine, and Motherhood*

Women's birth stories—like our bodies—struggle against cultural conditioning, paternalism, and the tensions wrought by sexism and sex differences. It is so important that we keep telling them, as Case has done in *We Are Animals*, a satisfying, insightful journey through early motherhood that is kept grounded with fresh reportage and fascinating biological and historical findings.

— Jennifer Block, author of *Pushed: Why Health Care Needs a Feminist Revolution*

Drawing on her own experience, her wide reading, and her ample talents as a writer, Jennifer Case has produced a searing, illuminating account of motherhood in all its cultural and biological complexity.

— Scott Russell Sanders, author of *The Way of Imagination: Essays*

Eloquent, beautiful, moving, and profound.

— Andrew Solomon, author of *Far from the Tree: Parents, Children, and the Search for Identity*

WE ARE
ANIMALS

*On the Nature and Politics
of Motherhood*

~ • ~

Jennifer Case

TRINITY UNIVERSITY PRESS
San Antonio

For anyone who needs it,
especially mothers of young children

Trinity University Press
San Antonio, Texas 78212

Image credits: page 143, *Scientific American*, January 24, 1872; page 146, New York Public Library Digital Collections; page 150 and page 154, United States Patent and Trademark Office; page 156, created by author; page 159, collage by author from images in Louis Fischer's 1903 *Infant-Feeding in Its Relation to Health and Disease* and Jean Bernard's 1816 sketch *Skull of Cow*.

Book design by BookMatters, Berkeley
Cover design by Anne Richmond Boston
Cover illustration by Julia Oldham
Author photo by Mike Kemp

ISBN 978-1-59534-301-7 paper
ISBN 978-1-59534-302-4 ebook

Trinity University Press strives to produce its books using methods and materials in an environmentally sensitive manner. We favor working with manufacturers that practice sustainable management of all-natural resources, produce paper using recycled stock, and manage forests with the best possible practices for people, biodiversity, and sustainability. The press is a member of the Green Press Initiative, a nonprofit program dedicated to supporting publishers in their efforts to reduce their impacts on endangered forests, climate change, and forest-dependent communities.

The paper used in this publication meets the minimum requirements of the American National Standard for Information Sciences—Permanence of Paper for Printed Library Materials, ansi 39.48–1992.

CIP data on file at the Library of Congress

28 27 26 25 24 | 5 4 3 2 1

CONTENTS

PROLOGUE

MESSAGE FOR THE ANIMAL MOTHER

You are teats-tingling, hairy line from your pubis to your belly button, stretched skin that has spread and then shrunk to create ripples and dapples. You are bite and aching neck and an arm that always reaches out and will hold a child when they need to be held and will grab that child when they need to be held back. When children hit their heads on a rock or a table or the thinly carpeted floor, you will run to them and hold ice to the pulsing bruise, and in the back side of your left cheek a bulge of your own will burgeon. You are power, though you do not always know it. You are sparks and mirror neurons and a life force throbbing to reach the future.

But sometimes you forget this. Sometimes you lie in bed, or wish you were lying in bed, or wander through the rooms of a dark house, a dark cave. Sometimes you push your fingers deep into rocky clay soil, so deep you cut your finger on stone, and still the barb at the back of your chest is a barb, and still your mind is full of voices that conflict. Something pulls you elsewhere, and something holds you here, and you do not know which is the better choice, and so you stay.

Mothers have lost themselves in this space. Hands on children.

Hands in the sink. Hands in water turning red and then clear and then frothy. Mothers have brushed their children's hair and seen their own selves spiraling upward, like the strands of a spider web, filaments floating and breaking in a breeze. A snail crawls across red bricks on the sidewalk, grit on grit. A blue egg cracks in the gutter. Where are you now?

Once you were young, and like all of us, naïve, and this is how it always is, so don't beat yourself up. Once you thought motherhood wouldn't be bristle, the sharp knob on the back of your neck, the sharp throb of a nerve two inches right of your left armpit. Once you thought motherhood meant family-hood, or something like that, forgetting that it was you who was the mother—you alone, mouth open and then clenched on a dark and throbbing night.

Do not believe this is anyone else's story. Do not believe this is anyone else's choice. When you stare into the lake or the river or wipe the mist from the smoky mirror, you will only see yourself.

Oh, mother. You don't believe me. I see you caving in, like a carcass, so full of fear you've already made yourself dead. I see you eyeing the white cloth, the small sock, the twisted clasp of the bra. You don't believe me that the anger in you is part of being a mother. You don't believe you will remain a mother just the same. You don't believe that the eye-flash, hiccup, aching longing to be elsewhere is one and the same with the hug so tight you feel your child's bones.

Oh, mother. The time will come when the belly will glisten and the sky will open and the mud will seep to your ankles. The time will come when the den is empty and the nearly grown daughter will stand at your side. The time will come when the leaves crackle a message and you will let go of the things you need to let go of, and your body will lighten so much you will fly.

But until then, lean close and listen. Hear the fervent scratch in my voice. In the deep folds of your pelvis, in the center of that hardened fist, you have always known the answer. You have always made the choices you needed to make. You are not stupid. And when the next choice comes, you will gather yourself—milk, bones, and bristle—and you will go.

WE ARE ANIMALS

Four days before my daughter is born, I am at the ob-gyn clinic for a usual, now weekly exam. The nurse straps the blood pressure cuff around my biceps. I breathe slowly, in and out, breathing in calmness, even though I can already see the nurse's frown out of the corner of my eyes. "Hmm," she says, like she has at each appointment for the past month. "It's high. Have you been feeling okay?"

I nod, as I always have. Though my blood pressure has been rising, I drink plenty of water and do not cross my legs. I assume it is just tension: white coat syndrome. When my midwife takes my blood pressure, it is always lower. I ignore the nurse's comment and focus instead on the flickering lights, on the posters of fetuses gestating, bigger and bigger each month. I allow myself to now, finally, look at the last image: the infant almost fully formed.

I am waiting there, for my midwife's quiet knock, when the exam room door bursts open and my midwife snaps, "We're done." Tall and thin, about the same age as me, her head nearly touches the doorway. Her eyes are focused and fierce, her voice tight.

My first thought is that she is firing us. She doesn't want to work with us anymore. My husband and I have to get out.

"We can't have you walking around with a blood pressure of 150 over 100," she says. It takes a few moments for me to realize that she means the baby. She means it is time for the baby to come out. As in now. As in today.

In the exam room I've sat in again and again and again, the exam room that has become familiar to me these past eight months, where Katie has praised us for being calm and for taking everything as it comes, an anxiety that I've spent nine months repressing swells into my throat.

Katie talks about induction. About wheeling us to labor and delivery.

I do not hear because I am crying. I do not want to be induced. I know inductions often lead to epidurals, and epidurals to C-sections, and I want neither of those things. Instead, I want to trust my body and let my body do its work. Yet here the nurses are with the wheelchair, ready to wheel me to labor and delivery.

"No, no, no," my body says, my face says, though the only words that come out are tears.

I am crying in the exam room while my husband stares, surprised, openmouthed.

I am crying in the exam room, wondering what my midwife thinks of me now.

Prior to the birth of my daughter, the only medical procedure I'd had was oral surgery: the removal of my wisdom teeth. For someone who rarely allowed herself Tylenol, I was curious about anesthesia. What would I notice? What would I "dream" of? What would I remember of that shift out of consciousness? Of the shift back in?

The morning of that surgery, I considered myself an investigator. I took mental notes as the nurse prepared the IV and explained the procedure. I observed the cabinets in front of me, the tray full of instruments on the counter, the window to the left with its thick blinds.

When the nurse anesthesiologist inserted the IV, I felt my body loiter behind me. The nurses talked among each other. The oral surgeon walked in, washed his hands, and slowly straightened tools on the counter.

Two of the nurses began to laugh. "Do you think Dr. Luke is handsome?" they asked. I was nineteen years old, splayed on a dental chair wearing sweatpants and an old T-shirt. I wondered what prompted the question. What expression was plastered on my face?

I did not think he was cute. He was a man in the corner of the room with a mask covering his mouth and nose. Nothing more than that. But my lips were numb. My body was numb. I was floating two feet above the chair.

"You do, don't you," they said, all of them chuckling by then.

I tried to respond—to reach out through the drifting and lifting of my body on the chair—but I had no way to respond, no way to correct them, besides the faint shaking of my head, which only caused them to chortle more. And I hated them for that—for that teasing. For my inability to correct their strange and immature assumptions.

Trusting one's body and trusting medical institutions are two different things, but for years and years I hated them. Even today, I hold a grudge.

Is it a flaw? Is it a flaw to not want to turn yourself off?

~•~

In labor and delivery, the nurses have me lay on my side. They watch my blood pressure for an hour. I breathe slowly and purposefully and try not to imagine what the rest of the day might bring. Shortly after lunch, my midwife comes in, along with another midwife and the head nurse. My blood pressure has fallen enough, and my lab results don't show signs of preeclampsia. "You need to stay on bedrest over the weekend and come in for a nonstress test Monday morning," my midwife says, "but let's hope you go into labor on your own over the weekend."

My husband works Friday and Saturday. Before he leaves in the morning, he stacks DVDs on the coffee table in front of me, fills my Nalgene with water, and adds a lemon. "Take a nap," he tells me, because I slept poorly that night—awake at 2 a.m. with contractions that kept up with faint regularity before disappearing with the rising sun.

I lay on my side on the futon. My husband kisses my forehead. Worry fissures his face. He hesitates. "Do you need me to stay? Do you have a friend who can come over?"

"I'll be fine," I tell him. "I'll let you know if you need to come home."

Slowly, he leaves. The door clicks behind him. The car rumbles as he backs out of the driveway.

I lay on the futon, a hand on my overstretched belly. I push "play" on the DVD's remote, and then I push "stop."

"This is silly," I say.

I hoist myself up. I slice onions and peppers in the kitchen. I make a batch of chili in the Crock-Pot. I walk a mile through the park behind our house. Walking, I know, is supposed to induce labor. If the baby needs to come out, I might as well help.

"Are you resting?" my husband texts.

"Yes," I respond, though I am outside. It is cloudy, thirty-one degrees. I pause at the top of a hill, the tennis courts and baseball field below me. I welcome the sting of the air.

These are the expectations I have: if I keep walking, if I keep doing prenatal yoga, if I eat healthy, I will be fine.

If I keep walking, if I eat healthy, I won't gain too much weight, I'll stay in relatively good shape, the baby will be healthy, and my body will be ready for labor. I will be fine.

If I do what I need to, I'll have a natural birth experience. I won't need an epidural. I won't need a C-section. I won't be stuck in a hospital bed, unable to feel my legs. I will be fine.

If I do what I need to, I will stay in control. My body will remain strong and capable. I will be fine.

Upon learning of my daughter's December 20 due date, a friend who works in a maternity ward warns me of the holidays. "They'll probably pressure you to have a C-section," she says. "I see it all the time. They don't want you going into labor on Christmas."

I tell another friend, who also had a holiday due date, that I'm worried.

"Oh, I felt the same way at first, but it's not so bad," she tells me. "They scheduled both C-sections, I went in, I had the babies, and I was back in the gym within two weeks. They had it completely controlled."

Which is precisely what I'm afraid of.

I do not have a birth plan, but if I thought of what I wanted, what I really wanted, it would be this: I'd notice labor starting. Hardly perceptible at first, like the flutter of my daughter's kicks, which I didn't recognize for what they were until a nurse pointed them out on the sonogram, said "I can't believe you don't feel that," and I suddenly connected the palpitations with the movement of my daughter's limbs. Yes, labor would start like that—hardly a transition between life before and life after, just an easing in. Labor would get stronger, of course, and I would pace, and go on a walk, and cook. I would fill the day with all that I needed to, all I was supposed to do, until I absolutely had to go to the hospital. I wouldn't be one of those women who turn up at the hospital only to be sent home with a smile and a pat on the head because she isn't far enough along.

No, I would be smart about it. I would be knowledgeable. And once at the hospital, I would use the birth ball, or the tub. I would pace the halls, letting my body do what it needed to. Giving my body time and space. And when the time finally came, I would squat rather than lay on my back, and who knows how it would be, but I would feel it and be patient with myself. At each step, I'd feel it and be aware.

When my blood pressure is once again high the Monday after my weekend of bedrest, my midwife, for the second time, tells me it is time to induce. For the second time, the nurse insists I sit in the wheelchair, pushes me out the back "privacy" exit of the clinic, across the hallway, through a series of corridors, and into the elevator that leads to the labor and delivery ward.

For the second time, I am with women I do not know, in a hospital room, and they are hooking me to machines, taking my blood pressure, asking me to change into a hospital gown so well washed the worn ties won't stay over my shoulders.

And though I am more prepared—have braced myself all weekend for the possibility of induction—for the second time, I am crying. Silent tears that I cannot stop. That I can't understand.

I am crying as the nurse tries three times to insert my IV. I am crying as the blood pressure numbers flicker on the screen. As the various sensors for fetal heartbeat are stuck to my abdomen. As the nurse tells me to stay on my side to lower my blood pressure, which has jumped to 160/110. "You look like you're going to melt into a puddle of tears," she tells me, checking my numbers, strapping things on, taping the IV tighter to my arm.

And I want to say, "This is not who I am," yet who am I in this room, connected to these monitors? Blood pressure rising and rising and rising?

A friend of many years, a friend who I have long admired for her ferocity and professional drive, sends me an essay she's written about sex. In the essay, she calls herself "the great observer" and admits she didn't have an orgasm until she was in her late twenties. Though sex was pleasurable, she just was hardly ever fully in her body. She says she wondered if she was flawed. She says she wondered how she could make her body cooperate.

I read the essay and nod and want to say, "Yes! I know! I know! I keep myself awake by thinking, I don't let myself get drunk, and sometimes, during sex, I find myself preoccupied by other things. How many of us are out there in the world?"

Instead, I pause. What would such revelations reveal about my ability to embrace my full, animal self?

I pause, unable to admit to such things.

For a year, I work with high schoolers who can't control themselves. Almost every day, someone has a panic attack or an attack of anger. They lose control of their bodies—throwing books, punching holes in the walls, spitting—their eyes fierce and wild with anger, but even more with fear. I talk in a steady, calm voice, ask questions, ask how they feel, until they calm and slump against a wall. And only then do I notice that my heart, too, is racing, though my voice has not risen.

I wonder, in those moments, what it is like to lose control. What it is like to not care who is watching. I wish that once, just once, I could let myself manifest whatever it is I am feeling—whether anger, sadness, or ecstasy—rather than shy away, cut myself off. Rather than go on long walks, or write in my notebooks. Rather than turn from my husband, squeeze my eyes shut, and isolate myself until whatever it is I am feeling can be contained.

I am on the birth ball. The contractions come with regularity. My husband presses a hand into my lower back. Harder, I tell him. I bounce, slowly, on the ball, move my hips back and forth as the tightening takes over. I let the tightening flow into the ball, let the tightening meet my husband's fist, pressing so hard it will leave a bruise the next day, though I don't sense that, then. I like the ball. The contractions come and go, and I joke with my husband between them, and I feel in control. My legs are strong. My lower abdomen is a solid, strong rock as it contracts and tightens.

But then the nurse comes in. "It's been twenty minutes and your blood pressure is up," she says. "Let's have you get back into bed and on your side."

I want to tell her no. I want to say, "I'm just fine here." What is it about these cream walls, these metal bedframes, that stops me?

I get back into the bed. I lay on my side. The contraction comes, and this time my belly is in front of me, unattached. My husband's fist is in the wrong place. Too high. I want to tell him to move it, but the pain clamps my mouth. I am riding it out. I am waiting. I am a knife that wants to cut my way out of this place.

For years growing up, images of sex unnerve me: humping bodies, moans, grasping—undiluted desire so visible, for all to see.

When I am in high school, I come upon a mallard mounting a female duck. He clamps his beak around her neck. He is driven, all attention toward one single focus. He has pulled out her feathers. They are splayed around the grass and hang, half-detached from her neck. One hangs from just above her eye. She is ragged. In her dilated iris, I see only fear.

In college, my boyfriend and his roommates keep a photograph of fornicating llamas on an end table in the living room. They took it at a campground. One llama is on top of the other llama in a sandy square. In the side of the photograph, children point.

My boyfriend shows me the photograph the first time I visit his apartment. He and his roommates laugh. They want me to laugh, too.

"That's a little immature," I say.

I say it again a few months later to the plastic dinosaurs that line the basement rafters at his parents' house. One dinosaur mounting another, the tightness of their plastic legs holding them together for years, so that when you pick them up, they leave dusty outlines.

That night, after my boyfriend and I have watched movies, letting the subterranean darkness of the room and the volume of the television cover up our own silent shiftings—after footsteps on the stairway make us freeze, and laugh, and stop—after my boyfriend, who will become my husband, returns to his bedroom one floor above, and I am left on the daybed in the basement, I take the dinosaur couplings apart.

Leave them alone, I want to say. *Give them their privacy. Don't look and laugh.*

At 3 p.m., two and a half hours after they break my water, I am only four centimeters dilated and 80 percent effaced. My midwife tells me that if I continue dilating one centimeter an hour, I may need an epidural later, to relax and speed the process. She ups the Pitocin.

The contractions are strong enough that I have to breathe through them. Katie speaks to me between pauses. She says she is going to grab some dinner and will come back. I feel stuck. Stuck in this bed. Stuck on my side. The Pitocin drips into my arm. I breathe and breathe and breathe.

At a state fair, when I am five months pregnant, we sit on bleachers in the cow birthing tent, and listen to her moan. She is on her side. Her moans come from deep within her. Somewhere so deep, it must be beyond her body. My daughter is a half-developed fetus inside of me. My husband pulls at his shirt, sweat seeping up the back. "It's hot in here. Are you ready to leave?" he asks.

The cow is moaning, people are moving in and out of the tent. Blood from a previous birth stains part of the floor. Or I think it is blood. Not fully swept up or covered with straw. I stare at the cow. I watch her. Kids who do not know what is happening watch her. Teenagers who know but do not know what is happening watch her. They take photographs that they'll perhaps mock and jeer in college dorm rooms.

At the side of the tent, a day-old calf—the one that left the blood?—naps in a pen of straw. Children reach their hands toward it. The calf's hair is soft and velvety. The mother is nowhere in sight.

In the main pen, in the middle of the birthing tent, the cow's eyes are glazed. Her mouth is open. And is it fear I see? Pain? I do not know. But there she is. Alone and on such terrible display. What is she looking at? What does she see?

"It will be a few hours. Maybe even a day," the veterinarian says. People wipe their foreheads. They sigh and leave.

"Are you ready to go?" my husband asks again. I cannot turn away.

Four months later, I am in a hospital room. The room is quiet, but in the hallway: scurrying. Nurses move back and forth. A door opens and closes, opens and closes. And each time: the moaning. The deep moaning. Inhuman in its depth. Uncontrollable. Like old, ancient air, expelled from the lungs. I listen and want to turn away, want the walls to be thicker. I listen and want to follow the sound—to pull my IV with me through the hallways and see what she is doing. I listen, transfixed. I can't focus on anything else.

I do not remember the moment it ended. I do not remember an after. I do not remember if that was me.

Why am I afraid of losing control?

Maybe I won't seem as put together. Maybe I will seem needy and scared.

Maybe I *am* needy and scared.

Maybe I will no longer seem like someone with answers. Someone who knows what she is doing and what she wants. And if I don't know what I am doing and what I want?

I will get trampled. Violated. I will not be able to control what others see.

I do not want anyone to judge and belittle me.

I do not trust anyone enough not to judge.

The contractions seem to come close together. I hardly have a moment to unclench my hands from my husband's arm, from the edge of the bed, before I can feel the tightening begin again in my back. My ball of a belly becomes a muscle of its own, hard as a rock. It clenches. The Pitocin causes it to clench, tighter and tighter.

"There's hardly a pause," I say, breathless. "Isn't there supposed to be a break?"

The nurse, whose name I do not recall, hardly heard when she first said it, says something about the contractions coming back-to-back and double-peaked, which sometimes happens with Pitocin, and she'll see if she can lower the dose. Her words skip on waves and slow in the water, sinking to my bed like flat stones.

The world is water. The air thick and humid and wet, sounds and people far away from where I am, my body, this clenching. I resort to "he he hoos," the only breathing technique I can remember from the classes we took, the only breathing that seems to make sense. The lights dim. The faint beeping of monitors fades away. *He he hoo. He he hoo.*

Do you need pain medication? someone asks through the fog and the water.

Heeeeee. Heeeeeeee. Hooooooooooooo, I say, my face closed, my eyes closed. I cannot answer her. I just breathe. Even between the contractions, I can't answer. I close my eyes and rest, and sometimes look into my husband's face, which takes up the entire room, dissipating on the edges, not quite there at all, as if the world will disappear any minute. *He he hoooo. He he hoooo.* All experience exists in that sound, all consciousness, and though the image is there—my husband's face—I am not.

Once, I fell asleep in a park in Paris. The day was warm. There was live music. My friend and I had lain down on the grass. We'd been walking all day, miles and miles and miles. My feet tingled with joy. The sun was pleasant on my face. I closed my eyes, let the warmth soak in. Let the sun make an orange glow of my eyelids.

"Jennie. Jennie," my friend said, a hand on my shoulder.

My friend's profile formed a shadow in my vision. Her hair fell inches from my face. The sun was a halo in the sky.

"You fell asleep. I don't want you to get sunburned."

And it was awe, more than anything else, that stayed with me. That I had embraced that warmth. That I had let myself fall asleep. That for however long my friend had let me sleep, I didn't know where I was. Didn't know I was in a park, vulnerable and surrounded by strange people, in the middle of Paris.

I mention, breathless, to the shadows and the darkness in the room, that I am feeling downward pressure. The nurse whose name I do not know and whose hair color I never see says I am seven centimeters dilated, and then eight centimeters, and then fully dilated. I note her surprise through the fog and water. The pressure increases, inching forward. My body clenches and shudders as I am on my side.

Don't push, I hear through the water and the fog.

Wait for Katie, don't push, just breathe.

As if it is possible to not obey my own body, to tell it to wait, to stop. As if I can halt the shuddering sensation, me on my side in the fetal position, my legs curled and bent, my knees as close to my round belly as I can get them.

An oxygen mask appears over my face. I breathe into it. *He he hoooo*, still. I do not open my eyes to look at my husband. The air enters my nose. A hand presses against my back. Another hand, my own, clenches the oxygen mask. I breathe into it, *he he hoooo*: two quick cutting breaths and then the long exhale.

Don't push, don't push, they say.

Where is Katie, I reply, a voice so strained my husband will later say it broke his heart.

Someone else holds the mask over my face, I grip the edge of the bed, my body shudders, and I cannot stop it, I do not try to stop it, my knees pulled up, rocking, twitching, the downward pressure moving down and down and down. I cannot hold back the urge to push. I don't hold back the urge to push.

People move around me, talk about the on-call doctor. I shudder and flip on the bed. Like a fish, like an animal, like a body, and whether labor started with Pitocin or not, I know I have moved beyond them. I know I have left this place. The room dark, dark, dark. The oxygen mask. I could be anywhere. I am not here. I am *here*. *We* are here. Here in this breath, this body, surrounded by shuffling and breath and air, by gripping and clenching and urging. The cutoff moan of an inability to hold back. *Put that energy toward pushing*, someone says, and then it is silent. Silent pushing through heat and tissue, tissue stretched so tight it's fire, and ripping and darkness and air until suddenly it stops and I break out in sweat and there she is, a wet, squirming being with wrinkles in the folds of her elbows and knees, red and clenched on my chest.

"Oh," I say. "Oh." Because we are animals after all.

Is that what people feel when they are drunk? When they let their bodies melt into a bed and shift into sleep? When they lose themselves in meditation? When my friend, in her late twenties, first let go of herself during sex? When my students at the alternative high school let go of themselves and became fistfuls of rage?

When we let go of the need to control our physical and emotional selves, does the world around us disappear? Or do we simply become part of something larger?

Afterward, when we are telling the story of our daughter's birth to family and friends, my husband will look at me with pride, with amazement. "You pushed her out like it was nothing," he'll say. "You just popped her out."

And I won't know how to respond.

In his eyes, there isn't revulsion. Only wonder. Only awe.

Yet, it didn't feel like nothing. She didn't just pop out. It was the most difficult thing I've ever done in my life. I sometimes wonder if, looking down at myself in those moments, I would have been appalled at the angular shifting and turning, the pain slick on my face, the deepness of that one, single moan. But I wasn't. I couldn't be. I was caught up in something, caught somewhere, and trying to understand that space is an exercise I don't need to explicate.

All I know: in the hours and days afterward, when my body ached with what it had done, even as the memories and sensations slipped away, I didn't care what my husband saw. What the nurses and midwife saw. What another woman, strolling the hallway of that maternity ward, saw. It simply did not matter. My body had claimed me, and the only thing I felt was power.

BABYCENTER

AN ESSAY ON PLACE

My husband wouldn't be home for another six hours, and already the day felt like it would never end. I wiped peanut butter from my daughter's face and ran through the list of ways to entertain her. We'd read stories until my throat had dried up. She'd jumped in her jumper. We'd folded the diapers and built towers from blocks. We couldn't go on a walk until the rain stopped. And it was too early in the day to FaceTime with my mom. Which left…what? Nothing. I carried my daughter to her play mat in the living room and—in a movement that had become all too familiar—reached into my back pocket and pulled out my phone.

The first post on the BabyCenter discussion board—part of a megalithic parenting site owned by Johnson & Johnson—was from Crazymama2.[1] Over the previous few days she had been spotting off and on, and in the past twenty-four hours her post had expanded into a play-by-play of her evening and night:

5:34 P.M.: Ugh so I spotted a small amount of pink on Tuesday and just had more today. It seems to have stopped and turned light brown but so scary to see nonetheless….Took a test and it is looking good but dang I just need a non-spotting pregnancy after my two CP[.][2] I'm so over being scared ☹

6:40 P.M.: Dr. called wanted me to go to the er for evaluation
ugh yea me

7:35 P.M.: Just checked in waiting to be called back. Going to be
a long night blah

8:55 P.M.: Waiting to have blood work and ultrasound. They
won't check progesterone they said they don't do that in the
ER. Boo. I haven't had any more spotting. It was just some pink
when I wiped and then a little light brown and now nothing for
the past 4 hours.

9:30 P.M.: Just had my u/s.[3] She couldn't say much but she said
to ease my mind she saw the yolk sac but no fetal pole yet which
is expected since I'm only 5 weeks and 1 day. Waiting on labs.

12:16 A.M.: Hcg[4] was in the 3200 range and ultrasound is
consistent w my dates all looks good.

I scrolled to the end, through the upbeat "hang in there"s
that others left, and Crazymama2's "thanx"es and "lol"s. The
thread contained more than fifty posts. In each one, I could feel
Crazymama2 reaching out, desperate for attention. There was
something unnerving about her neediness. I imagined her using
thumbs to type message-board posts while sitting on a cot in the
ER, the curtain drawn, nurses and doctors scuttling outside to
gunshot victims and those suffering from heart attacks. If it was
a miscarriage, nothing at five to six weeks could stop it. *Accept the
truth*, part of me wanted to say. *Keep it to yourself. Do you realize
how pitiful you sound?*

Yet I was obsessed. In the quiet of our apartment, rain hitting
the windows, I followed Crazymama2's posts. I kept logging
back in to BabyCenter, as I had throughout my pregnancy and

daughter's early months. What if Crazymama2 had no one else to talk to? What if she had nowhere else to share her fears? More importantly: what if I didn't, either?

For a long time, my BabyCenter habit perplexed me. Before having a child, I considered myself a place-based advocate and was proud to shop at local stores and farmers' markets. I spent my autumns planting garlic at urban farms and raking leaves for neighbors, while in the spring I participated in community efforts to clean trash from the river. When my husband and I went on vacations, we visited state parks, and my shelves were filled with books by Scott Russell Sanders and Wendell Berry. I believed that if I cared for my community, the people and place would in turn sustain me. In contrast, I shunned the isolated pull of cyberspace, which I feared would remove me from the world.

Once I became pregnant, however, my use of technology changed. I couldn't keep myself away from social networking sites. Suddenly, I stalked the photos pregnant strangers posted each month of their bellies, their hands around that growing weight. I translated threads full of acronyms I had never seen before. STTN. DH. CIO. POAS. EBF. BLW.[5] I sat, both hypnotized and repelled, as I read stories of inductions, episiotomies, and front-to-back third-degree tears.

Later, when my daughter fell asleep nursing and a book was too far from reach, I continued to spend hours on my phone scrolling through BabyCenter's online forums, comparing my daughter's length and weight, and her nap and sleep patterns, against statistics posted by others on her birth board. I flipped through pictures of other children, amazed my daughter was growing at the same rate as all of them.

Unknowingly, I was participating in a larger trend. In March

2012, three out of four mothers visited Facebook. New mothers spend approximately three hours a day on the internet, and in "Digital Motherhood," a study from the United Kingdom, Lorna Gibson and Vicki Hanson write, "Overwhelmingly, mothers cited their ownership of mobile phones, specifically smart phones, as one of the best tools for a modern mother."

I certainly used my phone as a tool, but I also used it to fill out the days. And this is where my participation in BabyCenter most concerned me. Shouldn't motherhood be defined by the connections and the community I was forming in person, both with my baby and with other moms? Before having my daughter, I'd imagined early motherhood as a constant stream of visitors: friends offering to do dishes, neighbors coming by with casseroles, family stopping by so that I could take a nap. I'd imagined that I'd experience firsthand the oft-quoted phrase "it takes a village," and that having a child would ground me even more firmly in place.

Instead, as my daughter cooed on her play mat, batting at a toy I held in front of her face, I turned to my phone. The afternoon had been long, my husband wouldn't be home for another hour, and I was bored, bored, bored. I flipped through threads on how to entertain infants. Threads about the challenges of returning to work. Threads about how to arrange good childcare. I felt vaguely guilty for not paying complete attention to my daughter. I searched for updates from Crazymama2. Fifteen minutes later, I forced myself to put the phone down.

Which isn't to say I didn't interact with other mothers in person. When our babies were five months old, two mothers and I met for a walk in the park. We were graduate students at the local university. Our eagerness for socialization—even if it meant loading the stroller, packing the diaper bag, and trying to time a gathering around tenuous nap schedules—shone on our faces. We beamed when we saw each other.

Yet our conversation was halting. Unlike the mothers I met online, who did not hold back their opinions—"We are a bunch of hormonal women. Be prepared for drama," BabyCenter users often wrote in response to disagreements—the mothers I met in person guarded the decisions they'd made about breastfeeding, diapers, and day care.

Early in our walk, Carla yawned and complained about the lack of sleep. In response, Allison shared that she and her spouse had used the Ferber method of sleep training with their son. "It was hard the first three nights, hearing him cry, but things are so much better now."

"Oh," Carla said. "I would never do that."

We stiffened and walked in silence for a block.

I realize, now that my daughter is three, how profoundly isolated I felt as I transitioned into motherhood. Those first few weeks, the rules for my recovery forced me into a quasi-quarantine that overwhelmed me: Do not carry more than twenty pounds for two weeks. Do not walk more than a couple of blocks. Do not exercise to the point of increased bleeding. Irrigate the stitches with a squeeze bottle and apply chilled witch hazel pads. Watch for clots. Take twice daily sitz baths to speed the healing process. And that was just for a vaginal birth, not a C-section—experienced by more than one-third of US mothers.

Then there's the baby. Hungry every two hours. Each breastfeeding session took at least a half hour those first few weeks, those first few months, really, which left an hour and a half of free time during which I wasn't stuck in a rocking chair, stuck on the couch, leaning against pillows in bed. But that hour and a half wasn't consistent. Sometimes it was one hour. Occasionally two. Before I felt comfortable nursing in front of others—before I'd mastered the tank top–T-shirt combination that allowed me to nurse without revealing to the world my own fumbling—scheduling visits or outings within those one-and-a-half-hour increments felt well beyond me, a logistical nightmare too complex for my sleep-deprived self.

And then there's the geographical isolation. To attend graduate school, I had moved from the Midwest to a postindustrial city in upstate New York. My parents lived two layovers away by airplane or, if they drove, sixteen hours by car. Friends of mine with children lived in other states; no one in my immediate social circle in Binghamton had children. A sibling couldn't pop over to babysit as my aunt had done for my mother. Nor, like my parents, did I live in a residential development where friends and neighbors were having children at the same time. My husband and I, like so many others who have moved for professions and jobs, had to create that support ourselves. In addition, the city we lived in just didn't cater to young parents with values similar to ours. Though Ithaca, one hour northwest, supported a cloth-diaper store that hosted free mother groups and breastfeeding classes, Binghamton's mother-child programming focused on basic needs.

According to sociologists Jodi Cohen and Jennifer Raymond, my experience isn't uncommon. "Demographic trends," they report, have "eliminated home-based communities in which women were primarily at home, raising children, and could rely on this propinquity for advice. As neighborhoods are no longer filled with women and young children interacting through the day, these geographic networks are lost and so is the informal support that was once afforded to pregnant women."

It's an attractive image: urban or suburban neighborhoods, women gathering at the park, meeting for walks, sharing stories over tea, at the meat counter of the butcher, pushing children in swings. If they had a question, all they'd have to do is look outside their window, walk across the hall, and someone could answer. Young girls would grow up with women around them, they'd see other young families at church, at community gatherings, and they would have grown up with those women, those families. Never a drought of people to approach with questions. Motherhood—the possibility, the challenges, the joys—would always have been a thread in their communities, their lives.

Of course, fifty, sixty, one hundred years ago, those home-based communities painted so vividly in sociological studies and my imagination were likely not so ideal. The mobility and career opportunities women have today go hand in hand with female empowerment. Before the 1960s, women were expected to get married and have children. Today, most women don't stay at home when child-rearing, and voluntary childlessness, though still stigmatized, has become more accepted.

I am thankful for these choices. I'm thankful I've never been expected to stay at home. I learned quickly, in those early months with my daughter, how much I would have struggled with that role. I missed the intellectual stimulation that had brought me to a graduate program in Binghamton; my daughter alone wasn't enough to fulfill me.

But in this shift, from home-based communities to global mobility, I recognize that we've also lost something. Though our worlds have expanded, they don't always accommodate the biological need, especially when child-rearing, for close kinship in place. We haven't yet figured out how to fill that absence of community and intergenerational support. As a result, we feel disconnected from motherhood, from fatherhood. We do not always see parenting stories around us, and so we become disoriented when navigating our own—no directions, no stars in the sky to guide us through those long nights. We must search for alternative communities. For many of us, this means looking online.

In addition to the hours I spent on BabyCenter, I eased my own isolation by going on walks. Once or sometimes twice a day, I'd pack my daughter in her stroller and take mile loops around the park. I walked quickly, steadily, willing my daughter into a nap. Then I slowed and stared at the other mothers, pushing their own strollers. I nodded at them and smiled. I willed them to talk to me. I learned, later, that I was participating in an activity three sociologists from the University of Waterloo coined in 2013 as "stroller stalking."

Apparently, a whole pattern has emerged: young mothers, or not-so-young mothers—the age of motherhood moving up and up—will follow other mothers at the park. They spot another mother, another stroller, a kid that could be the same age as their own. They'll alter their walking paths and sidle up, wide-eyed. How are you? How old are your children? Such a beautiful day for the park, no? This blind, desperate search for "mommy dates," as the scholars call them, can lead to all sorts of interesting interactions.

In their twenty-three-page discussion of the activity, the sociologists conclude that the practice is "not terribly effective." They instead suggest certain social media sites. In particular, sites that balance online discussion forums with in-town meetups.

In doing so, they seem to point to the innate difficulty of carving out the community we seek in this world, the difficulty of balancing digital and physical support. BabyCenter was easy to participate in: all I had to do was log in. In-person gatherings were harder to devise. And yet I craved those, too, which is why, once a month throughout my daughter's first year, I attended the local La Leche League meeting. Some nights I hardly said anything at all. I just sat there in the basement of the library, nodding, nursing my daughter, comforted by the presence of others, other women with other children, who talked about what they struggled with, what they loved, what they feared about having more children—if the tongue-tie would cause latch issues again, or if they'd ever sleep through the night.

The conversations did not differ from those on BabyCenter, but here the support was embodied. We passed around colicky babies, giving the mothers a break, and when a recent immigrant who hardly spoke English propped her crying, spindly baby on her forearms, not knowing what to do, the La Leche League leader took her aside and helped her. A shirt was lifted. An infant latched under the fluorescent lights of the library.

I would never see that woman again. She left when the meeting ended that night and never returned. Yet I recognized myself in her: the struggle to find others, somewhere, who had also sat there, mouths agape at the tasks they'd been given, the tasks they'd said yes to, the tasks thrust into their arms.

When my daughter was eighteen months old, my husband and I began thinking about when, and if, we wanted to have another child. As had happened with our first, we discussed a date to try and conceive, and then the month came, and I second-guessed that timing and said, no, I'm not ready. I postponed the date— said we'd shoot for a summer due date instead. Nonetheless, I kept returning to BabyCenter. I checked the TTC[6] thread in the early morning, again during my break for lunch, and once more before bed. I was addicted. "Good night!" I would say, heading to the bedroom hours before my husband, only to curl on my side, alone with the threads. Who had POAS? Who had symptoms? Who was reconsidering the timing altogether, like my husband and me?

I watched and I wondered when I would try to conceive again; I watched and I wondered if I could ever become like the women who populated the TTC thread, women desperate for children, for pregnancy, women who ordered one hundred pregnancy tests so that they could take one every day starting at seven dpo.[7] They shopped in bulk on Amazon and eBay, and they had very strong opinions on which tests were best.

With my daughter, I used the cheapest test I could find: a blue-dye test from Target. It was a test that many of these women would never buy, women who swore by FRERs[8] but also stockpiled more expensive digital tests because of the satisfaction of seeing the word "pregnant." Even after they got a positive test, they kept taking FRERs, to see the progression of the lines, they said—a string of tests lined up side by side, that second meaningful pink mark getting darker and darker and darker as their pregnancies progressed, offering peace of mind against early miscarriages.

On the board, one woman posted that her period was late that month. She posted test after test after test—images captured with her smartphone, the test on the counter in her bathroom or held beneath the refrigerator's light to "bring out the line."

Each of her tests was blank to me. White as paper.

A few days later, she started spotting and asked if it was a chemical pregnancy, an early miscarriage. "Maybe," someone said. No one quite had the heart to tell her that she probably had never been pregnant at all. Such desperation. Such hopes. Part of me wanted to roll my eyes—to pass judgment. *Just accept that you are not yet pregnant*, I wanted to write. *This is not the time.*

I had the same reaction when WannaBMamma suddenly started posting tests three times a day: "I swear I see something. Another evaporation line? A vfbfp?[9] The picture isn't clear, but I swear it's there."

And then there was Chai, the thread "owner," who had maintained a luteal phase of five to six days for the past six months (rather than the ten days necessary for an egg to implant) but still wondered if spotting at six dpo could be implantation rather than the start of her menstrual cycle.

And I watched and read, and sometimes posted, but mostly watched as these strangers' lives played out on the screen. Because even though I would never become these women—I would never buy one hundred pregnancy tests and post the results online—the fact that they did gave me permission to view my body as important too. Worthy of monitoring. There could be a second child in our future. And although I would never say those words to my colleagues, to my friends, to my siblings—would never admit that I was calculating due dates and considering reducing my intake of caffeine—at least on the thread, I felt sane. At least on the thread, the intensity of my preoccupation with conception was shared. I wasn't some baby-crazy female, caught up in an irrational and easily belittled fixation, but part of a community: women aware of what female bodies could do. Women calculating their abilities, making plans. Setting their knife to the whetstone of what they were capable of—trying to claim some sort of control over what they wanted and the inherent unpredictability of the world: miscarriages, short luteal phases, cycles where the timing was right but nothing happened. Where the nothing that happened was balanced by that unspeakable hope.

I have come to respect the women who utilize sites such as BabyCenter, and yet when I think of them—of us—typing away on our smartphones, in the dead of night, or during breaks at work, or while a baby is nursing or happily swinging at a playground, what I come back to is aloneness. Why don't we find a way to ask these questions, have these conversations, and create these communities in person? Why, I ask myself, do so many women turn to online forums rather than the places and communities they participate in each day?

A friend suggests it might be gendered. In person, women guard themselves a little more than men do. Some of the research I've been reading about motherhood and social networking sites suggests that too. The aptly titled article "Digital Actualizations of Gender and Embodiment," published on the *Women's Studies International Forum*, analyzed mothers' posts on anonymous sites such as Reddit and concluded that women are socially "expected to perform 'fit pregnancy'" and that as bodies become more "leaky"—vaginal discharge, colostrum and milk, the night sweats of a body ridding itself of hormones—women tend to retreat from public spheres. They realize their animal bodies don't belong.

A few weeks before my daughter's due date, I remember looking in the mirror, at the fuller forearms, the fuller face, the protruding belly that made me waddle, made my crotch sting whenever I moved or tried to get out of bed. I stared at my tired eyes, thinking, *This is not how I see myself.* Yet I knew my distended abdomen was the first and often only thing others would perceive.

What do you do when the body you see in the mirror becomes, in a matter of months, a body you do not recognize?

What do you do when the new form your body takes on carries with it such strong cultural weight?

The sociologists who coined the term "stroller stalking" place motherhood and the use of social networking sites within the "age of anxiety," an era in which women are afraid of doing something wrong. There are high expectations yet less community, and so there is a "conspiracy of silence around ordinary motherhood": what it looks like, and how we are supposed to behave when nursing or when wheeling a crying infant through the grocery store. At the same time, Cohen and Raymond acknowledge that pregnancy itself is socially prescribed "as private, and therefore somewhat embarrassing to women, which encourages the dismissal of that lived experience as inappropriate for public discourse." The result is silence. Isolation. Women who feel compelled to perform a role in public that feels inauthentic.

Unfortunately, this even carries over into the medical field. At our hospital's childbirth class, when the instructor ran through pregnancy symptoms, how many people raised their hands at hemorrhoids? Incontinence? Only one, with gusto. The rest of us looked down, blushed, raised a hand halfheartedly—maybe a finger or two—a small flag of surrender in the air. We all felt ignored, a common experience that has been chronicled in the studies I now pore through in my attempt to understand my own attraction to BabyCenter. Our personal stories and experiences had been overlooked by the vast medical institution. And so we searched for information on our own. Information about our bodies, about the babies we would need to take care of, babies that we, as "good mothers" and "good patients," were somehow, inherently, expected to know so much about.

And this invisibility, perhaps, is why so many contemporary mothers have turned to social networking sites. It is why 89 percent of mothers post Facebook status updates about their children and why 96.5 percent post photos. It is why 91 percent of mothers use social media daily or weekly. It is why BabyCenter has 45 million monthly users. Users such as Crazymama2, WannaBMamma, and even myself. When asked why they use social networking sites, or what they do, the participants across these sociological studies have said that they search for answers to questions. They discuss limited or minimal support from family and friends. They say they feel isolated. Social media provides a way to obtain support. Ironically, it is online, where the body is concealed, or at least most controlled, that women can give voice to their bodies as well as their selves—to bring those competing identities back together.

Away from their actual lives—the rooms they move through, the people they know, the work they do for a living—they can stake out a voice and lay claim to their experiences, to see how their experiences and stories are interwoven in that longer, ongoing cycle of birth.

I haven't been on BabyCenter much lately. I've spent entire afternoons reading academic research about social networking sites and motherhood, yet I haven't returned to those sites. My daughter is in preschool and sleeping through the night. She has settled into a routine, which includes weekend playdates, and I've slowly developed friendships with other parents of young children. As I've grown more comfortable as a mother, I've also found it easier to return to and nurture the non-parenting support systems I have—support systems with other hikers, gardeners, and writers who think about environment and place.

Yet somewhere on BabyCenter, women are posting their basal body temperatures, asking for input on "possible faint lines," and sharing estimated due dates that they hold to their chests and clutch, like keys. They are asking about newborn feeding patterns and how to handle toddler temper tantrums. Their loneliness, joy, and desperation is palpable. *Is this normal? Are you experiencing this, too?* That *need* for community is there, an underground river, the current so strong it can carry us away.

And maybe it does. When I first discovered BabyCenter, I worried that the force of that river might pull me under. That in sucking me so fully into an online environment, I'd lose grip on the physical world. To a degree, I sometimes did. I don't want to know how many hours I spent on my phone during my daughter's infancy. But when it comes to the human need for kinship, nowhere else—perhaps not even in a home-based community—would I have encountered a group of women willing to share such intimate details about their private lives. Nowhere else would I have encountered more than ten thousand women with due dates in the same month as mine. Though I'd like to believe that we can work more purposefully as a society to strengthen our physical communities and support local networks, I also know that BabyCenter does not symbolize the cause of my isolation but rather a response to it. When I was desperate for connection, BabyCenter, as a location and a place, housed the community I needed to find.

NOTES

1. Usernames were changed to protect the identities of the mothers in this essay.

2. Chemical pregnancy. An egg is fertilized, but the pregnancy does not progress to the point where an ultrasound can pick it up.

3. Ultrasound.

4. Human chorionic gonadotropin, the hormone that pregnancy tests detect. In a healthy pregnancy, HCG doubles every twenty-four to forty-eight hours after a fertilized egg implants.

5. In order of appearance: sleep through the night, dear husband, cry it out (a form of sleep training), pee on a stick (take a pregnancy test), exclusively breastfed, baby-led weaning.

6. Trying to conceive.

7. Days post ovulation. Most pregnancy tests can't detect a pregnancy until at least twelve days post ovulation, though some women start testing around eight dpo.

8. First Response Early Result. A specific brand of pregnancy tests.

9. Very faint big fat positive.

ON CONTEMPLATING
A SECOND CHILD

The winter my husband and I debate whether to have a second child, I begin to carry around a photograph of my grandmother. The photograph is black and white, about three by four inches. On the back, in my grandmother's cursive, are the words *Omaha—Steve & Lori & 3 Neighbor Kids*.

The image is simple enough. My grandmother, with thin legs, a sleeveless pale blouse, large glasses, and a short, permed haircut, sits on a cement stoop in front of a house. She feeds a gangly baby a bottle, lifting her left foot just slightly to support the baby's back. To her right sit two girls. To her left a boy picks at his nose. In front, a near-naked toddler, who I assume is my father, turns and covers his ears.

I would overlook the image entirely if it weren't for my grandmother. Her furrowed eyes, her straight mouth, her slight frown. Though the children embody warm stoops and sunshine, my grandmother clearly is not happy, and I want to know why. Was it because she simply didn't want to be photographed that way: in the sleeveless blouse and shorts? Or is her discontent larger than that? Did she not want to be on that stoop, fenced in by kids? Their presence engulfs her, and I can't help but wonder if she felt stuck: my grandmother, the caretaker. My grandmother, who will later tell me she wishes she had gone to college before having children or even getting married.

I store the photograph in the pages of my journal, which I carry to and from the university where I teach. In the late afternoons, before I leave to pick up my daughter, I sometimes pull it out. Surrounded by those five children, my grandma looks tense and trapped.

The winter my husband and I debate whether to have a second child, I am a new faculty member at a state university. The job is a good one—the promising start of a long and hopefully reward-ing career—and yet our daughter is already three. I have six years to prepare for my tenure review; I have a year or two if we want another child close to her age.

Time condenses. I begin to look up articles on whether or not to stop after one child. I read about women who stop at one in order to have more time for their writing, themselves, and their mar-riages. I read about women who believe female academics pay a high price, that the system is unfair. One writer in the *Chronicle of Higher Education* says women should have more than one child if they want—and then admits she has two but no longer works in academia.

I had researched this topic when we were thinking of conceiving my daughter. I was a graduate student then, trying to figure out how to balance a family and a career. So much of what I read was fearful and negative, describing delayed career plans, discrimination and sexism in the classroom or from the administration. Women with children often tend not to get tenure or promotions. Many leave their jobs eventually. The outlook is grim, the writers said. I read the chapters, and my heart jumped a bit, and I gritted my teeth. But a child was what we wanted. I closed the books and turned away. I would do what I needed to do.

This time, I'm less certain. When I read of mothers who are happy and content with one child, I am relieved and happy. I think about all the things we can do now that our daughter is older, now that we don't have to consider pregnancy or another baby. We can go camping and kayaking. I have more time to write and connect with others. I have the energy to tend a garden and cook elaborate evening meals. I was so exhausted after my daughter was born, it took months for me to be able to do such things again: to juggle the nursing schedule with the time required to slice and sauté onions.

And yet, when I read articles by women who have had more than one child, I long for that, too. It's as if deciding not to have a second child is the same as saying no to parenthood in general. As if it means "I wouldn't do that again."

A female university professor gives this advice to me and a female friend at a conference: *Graduate school is a great time to have children.* The friend and I are both young and ambitious. We both are married and would like families. The advice buoys us, and we begin making plans.

A male university professor to me after I've accepted my first full-time, tenure-track job: *If you want two children, just go for it. Don't worry about timing.* I smile and nod. I say thank you. I wonder: Did he have to worry about timing? Did he have to worry about the exhaustion of pregnancy? About the way other faculty members would look at him before and after the child's birth—their embarrassed glances at his body and their doubt that he could juggle it all?

A female university professor to me, during my first year at my tenure-track job: *You won't be as productive when your children are young. But it will come back, after. And don't worry—you should still be able to get tenure even if you don't have a book.* Though she pauses, sympathetic. We both know there are no guarantees.

The winter my husband and I debate having a second child, I read an article about how the number of children our colleagues and friends have influences how many children we want ourselves. Peer pressure without our even realizing it.

Most of the friends I have in my profession have zero children or one child. A few have two. Most of the mentors I know have no children or two children. A few have one. My mother had three. My grandmother had four.

I tally up numbers as if they will tell me something. As if they can assure me of which choice I should make.

But they give me no assured answers. And my tallies ignore the most important variables: that having an infant means aloneness, and stalling, and mornings wrapped in sleeplessness, and less writing and connection for months on end. And most of all: exhaustion—a physical, draining exhaustion that is inherently biological—that neither better parental leave nor flexible childcare can relieve.

Most of the female colleagues I know who have published books have zero children. The males have zero children, or one child, or two children. Many, I realize, after thinking about it more, have two.

A female writer in a panel on motherhood and writing tells a room full of young mothers and aspiring mothers that each child you have is the equivalent of a book.

A friend asks me what it is that I—me, myself—want. I have trouble answering.

I do not want to disappoint anyone. My husband. My parents, anxious for grandkids.

I do not want to disappoint myself. But I also don't know what might disappoint me in the future. Not having another child? Or having another and realizing how much I gave up in the process?

Early motherhood, for me, was hushed. It was me in the apartment, alone, timing the day with feedings and walks outside when the weather was warm enough, counting down the hours until my husband came home. It was me, nursing my daughter, letting her fall asleep at the breast, so that I could adjust my shirt and reach for a book, turn the pages with my one free hand. I checked the books out from the library, where I'd put her in the Moby Wrap and sway through the aisles, just happy to be out of the apartment, near other people, never mind the quietness of the library and the strange smells from those who spent all day in front of public computers. I'd make my way to the child-rearing section and search, desperately, for books about mother-hood, books about what my life was turning into and what I had become.

I was like a person wrapped in a cocoon, a person contained by an infant, by the need to feed it, the need to sit there and rock, silently, for hours. I was a person, mouth closed, eyes open, mind wandering through the early mornings, the languid midday, the tepid afternoon, the uneven evening, when she'd cry for hours, the night broken by wails and nursing and shadows.

When I'd shower and let the water stream down my back, the days opened. I created such plans. But then her needs would beat them back, and my body, physiologically changed to serve and support her, could do nothing but serve her, and by the end of the day I was tired, tired, tired. Not unhappy, but tired.

And now she is three, looking more and more like a child. When she walks into our bedroom in the morning, just after the alarm has gone off, her head is higher than the top of my dresser. She is a new being, someone I do not know, and those old shadows of ourselves getting books from the library have eased back and dissipated. I reach for them; I try to see who I was. But when the child in front of me pulls my arm to get oatmeal and turn on "Elmo," that young mother, with her own goals and subdued desires, escapes my grasp.

Some of the graduate students I teach are considering children. The students are young and ambitious, bright with the future.

They want families and careers. I feel them watching me, glancing at my face and then at the photograph of my daughter on my desk. They watch me the same way I watched my own mentors, analyzing them as models of who I might be.

My students are conflicted. Scared. They worry motherhood will inhibit their writing. From their perspective, perhaps, it looks like I know what I'm doing. That I've carefully crafted my life. I want to pull them toward me and take off the mask. *Honey,* I want to say. *None of us knows what we're doing.*

At the dinner table, my husband and I discuss whether to have another child. Our daughter sits between us and asks for ketchup. We discuss whether to have another child when we go on walks and she holds our hands and we swing her over cracks. We discuss a second child at night, when we sit beside each other on the couch or next to each other in bed. The discussions go on and on and on.

My husband and I have a name picked out for the potential second child we may or may never have. It's the name of some opaque figure, some chubby-faced toddler I can see just behind my daughter, crawling and laughing and crying, sticking stickers on the wall and waking in the middle of the night. I can imagine an opaque second child in the high chair at our table, eating pureed peas and mango. I can imagine the child in our daughter's bright orange stroller, my hand a wooden limb at the edge of my vision, pushing that stroller around and around the block.

The child's face is fuzzy at the edges. It blurs in and out. And I do not know what this means. Are we dreaming? Are we stuck in a story whose conclusion has already been written? Will we soon wake up, tangled in bedsheets: our small family of three? The name of this potential second child like the dreams we all grow up with, spinning in our heads—middle school crushes, perfect jobs, recognition and accomplishments—dreams that carry us forward but that we eventually discard.

I have friends who struggled to conceive their first child. Friends who, in desperation, have turned to fertility treatment. Friends who've experienced miscarriages—so many miscarriages that they begin to talk about them in dead voices: *That's the miscarriage I had in the bathroom at work. That's the one when I went to see Lord of the Rings.* Friends who've had ectopic pregnancies and emergency surgery. I know people who have had stillborns. The stories go on and on and on. I lose my voice beneath them.

And then I have friends who realize, after one child, that they definitely don't want more, while others quit their jobs to become stay-at-home parents, and others try for a second child, again and again, without conceiving—forced to stop at one with resignation rather than contentment.

And then there's me. No strong desire either way, perhaps because when it comes to biology, and when it comes to culture and career, either way I am conceding.

I look at the photograph of my grandmother, surrounded by those five kids, and her slight frown. Her left foot lifts so that her knee can cradle the baby. Her arms ache in their steadiness. Sweat accumulates in her armpits and between her thighs.

Did her back hurt? Did she sit there on that stoop in the

summer and wonder what she was doing with her life—what other stories were possible, had once been possible, before her life eclipsed them?

My grandmother is lovely in that photograph. Her legs are slender. Her hair is permed and shapely. The collar of her white blouse falls open on her shoulders, and her forearms are toned from children and laundry.

She is young and she is youthful. I can sense the curve of her waist. The skin on her belly that has expanded and then sunk back in. She wears shorts that button at her hips and glasses that rest on the bridge of her nose.

The children beside her are children. They lift their shoulders and shrug and smile. And my grandma is there between them, in the background. Her not-smile is my own not-smile. I look at her and recognize a certain kind of pain.

When my husband and I first talked about marriage, we were in college. We were camping at a state park in early spring, and at night the temperature dipped so low we huddled into each other near the campfire, hips touching as the embers burned. We were in our early twenties, just learning who we were. We hadn't yet realized how hard life could be. In the night, with the embers, our tent, and the fire, our hips and shoulders creating their own heat, we imagined camping with children. We imagined bringing a family there. We built stories out of smoke and river and spring.

"How much do you want another child?" I ask my husband.

"A lot," he says.

"And if I don't? Would you still be happy if we only have one?"

He pauses. He half answers. His face crumples and turns sad.

What will make me happy? The question lingers; my lower lip dries and cracks from where I've curled it between my teeth. So many stories. So many terrifying choices.

Terrifying because sometimes, when it comes to stories, we only get one.

UNINTENDED

Before you even place it on the counter, the pregnancy test turns positive. You do a double take, sure that even though you are late by a week and had the slightest suspicion, the test's second blue line can't mean what it does.

When you found out you were pregnant with your first child, a child you very much wanted, your initial reaction was "oh, shit." You knew, when those two lines appeared, there was no turning back.

This time, the pattern reverses. For half an hour, the fact that you have gotten pregnant without trying feels like a miracle cupped in your hand. Then the doubts set in. All the doubts that had made you decide, just weeks ago, that one child would be enough. You sit on the toilet and lock the door. You fold over your legs and cram your chin between your knees.

That evening, your husband, who has always wanted another child, picks you up and spins you around and grins and talks about how cute the two children will be together, and whether the child will be left-handed or right, blonde or brunette, and how he thinks it will be another girl, and that will be lovely, and

how your parents will be thrilled, as will his. And his reaction is
perfect, though it does not match your own. You wish it matched
your own. When he grins, you grin back at him, but later he finds
you in the bedroom, curled in on yourself. You are crying, and you
cannot stop yourself from crying, and he asks why, and you tell
him, and he sets a hand on your shoulder and rubs your back and
lies by you as you tell him you are not excited about this child,
that you don't know what to do about that, that you are worried
about your career and your lack of excitement, and do you both
really want this pregnancy?

You do not at that moment say "abortion," but the word hovers
between you, glaring half-masticated above the door, swallowing
you along with it.

In the front of the yard, your husband and daughter wash the
cars. The hose spouts water. The blue bucket froths with suds. A
sharp light cuts their silhouettes from glossy paper, and when
your husband sprays her, your daughter squeals.

On the other side of the kitchen window, you levitate in darkness. Control has been wrenched from you. *Do you want this?*
doesn't even seem like a question you can ask. It has just happened. You didn't ask it to, but it has, and the only choice now is
how to respond.

Laughter warps and dims through the window. You imagine
your husband and daughter out there a year from now, a second
child in the carrier, batting at a toy in the shade. It would make
your husband's day: two children washing cars. A driveway. A
house.

It dawns on you: how small you are. How inconsequential.
You are a body reproducing your kind. That is all. You are a cog
in the play of evolution. For some reason, as for so many others,

you mistimed things, or the condom tore, or the pill didn't work, or the diaphragm and IUD didn't work, or the great hope didn't work, and the evolutionary will for new life broke through the barriers, not caring who you were, or what dreams you had, or what stories you were telling yourself about your life, and created a new one, all on its own. You are not in control. Your species is not in control. Everything is dictated by hormones. By the biological drive to reproduce. By the way parenting makes you the best and worst version of yourself. By the way you stare at your daughter, soaping the cars, and feel so deeply consumed.

You call your mother. Out of your mother's three pregnancies, two of them weren't planned. You call her and ask the question that has been haunting you: "How long did it take you to feel happy?"

With your brother, she answers, it took six months. With you, a bit shorter. Though it depended on the day. If your brother took a good nap, she looked forward to your arrival. If he cried and fussed, she doubted she could handle another.

She says she's excited for you. That it is normal to be scared. That you will adjust and be a good mother.

After you hang up, you trace the outline of a heart your daughter drew on the armchair and wonder how many women have been in this position before. Hundreds of thousands, you are sure. Millions. You imagine yourself one among those millions. You imagine all those silent voices. All those women, bracing for things they aren't sure they can bear.

You start to see infants everywhere: small babies held by mothers or fathers. They suckle and coo and cry as they're swaddled and rocked and strapped to their parents' backs.

Their parents look tired. But also joyful. The parents whisper into their children's ears before retreating like turtles into diaper-laden bags.

You start to smile at the babies. To note their cheeks. Their liquid eyes. The way they bounce and grin and drool and attempt to sit up despite their terrible, oversized thighs.

You catch yourself smiling. *You are not a feminist*, you say. *You are merely a woman who got pregnant. You are a coward. You are a sacrificial lamb.*

You attend your first appointment with your husband. The waiting room brims with women. Young women, in college, here for annual exams. White-haired women, seeking treatment for osteoporosis. Pregnant women with bellies of all different sizes, and one other woman, with her husband, perhaps newly pregnant like you.

You're not sure what to think right now about women's bodies. Whether you can love them. Instead you listen for your name. You strip and put on an open-faced gown. You place your feet in stirrups. You look at the ceiling rather than your husband, the doctor, the nurse.

You flinch.

It takes no time at all for the fetus to flicker on the screen. "And here's your baby," the doctor says, as the head, the body, and the four appendages immediately appear. Beneath it: the yolk sac. Around it, the thick, white lining of a uterus.

Everything measures well, and the doctor smiles, and you mimic her, and for a moment the wonder of it engulfs you: the fact that this fetus is growing, uninvited. The fact that your body is nourishing it without being asked.

"And look! There!" the doctor says, because at only eight

weeks—quite early, really—the ultrasound catches a quiver of arms and legs. A jiggle and dance. "This one is active."

She laughs and pauses, her hand still, while a fetus you can't feel moves inches beneath your skin. This will ask everything of you, you realize. It will ask everything of you. It will ask everything, and you will do what you can, and when it is born and they place it on your bare chest, and it nurses for the first time, you will disappear. You will feel pared down and mindless. You will question yourself. And yet there will be coos and smiles, a child learning who it is, a child growing up and experiencing its own grief. Anything and everything will happen, and it will break you. You know this, too. Staring at the ultrasound, you know this, as sure as anything. It will break you, like everything great and terrible in this life, and you will reassemble yourself. Because what choice do you have?—the doctor at your knee, your husband at your shoulder, the ultrasound wand pressed against your cervix?

What choice have any of you ever had?

A POLITICAL PREGNANCY

The spring that Trump wins the Republican primary, I discover I am pregnant with my second child. The pregnancy is unintended. A surprise. A month after I tell my husband I want to stop at one child, my urine on a stick reveals two blue lines.

My reaction isn't joy. I am deeply conflicted. But when I mention potentially terminating the pregnancy, my husband walks out of the room, refusing to discuss it.

"When you're a star, they let you do it. You can do anything. Grab them by the pussy. You can do anything."
—Donald Trump

I don't know what to do. Earlier that winter, when we were still debating a second child, my husband had leaned against the wall and said his purpose was to be a father. He wanted to volunteer as a troop leader and serve on the school PTO. He wanted clambering and laughter and a house ringing with children's voices. As he spoke, his face had opened, a small, trembling truth, and the fact that I no longer wanted a second child snared the space between us, so that it was me holding him back, me stopping him from fulfilling his vocation—me, the barrier between him and his life's fulfillment—and I thought, *This could break us. This, here, is the moment that could break us,* and that's what I think again, in the days after I pee on the stick, and my body has betrayed me, and I wonder if I can be the person who says no, who carves out of her body the child he wants, who commits an act that, in my husband's mind, will only ever be a sin.

I begin to lie on the couch and hold my breath against nausea. I stare at our family photo, hung on the opposite wall. In the photo, my daughter is four months old. She looks up at me, mouth open, while I prop her baby body with my hand. My husband leans over us both.

I inventory the belongings that fill our rented duplex: the books and mementos and matching T-shirts and coffee mugs. The rubber tubs of baby clothes, leftover from our daughter. A wave of nausea passes over me—metallic saliva. I reach for a cracker and shut my eyes to the world.

In the evenings, when I say, "I wish this weren't happening. I wish I weren't pregnant," my husband says, "I know," or he says nothing, or he rubs my back until I am silent and spent.

When I say, "I'm not excited for this child," he says, "I'll be excited for both of us," and something inside of me shrivels and cracks, because what does that mean for him to be excited enough for both of us? For me to become the body carrying a child others want?

I do not want to be pregnant, but I don't want to hurt my husband, and since I can't *not* have the child without hurting my husband, the pregnancy continues.

"It must be a pretty picture, you dropping to your knees."
  —Donald Trump

That summer, my blood volume increases by 50 percent. My breasts double in size. A brown "mask of pregnancy" appears on my chest. I succumb to exhaustion by 2 p.m. every afternoon. I grow dehydrated quickly. I watch my blood pressure tick up, like it had when I was pregnant with my daughter. I must stop to catch my breath after climbing a flight of stairs. By the end of September, the muscles on my abdomen separate from one another. They leave a chasm around my belly button that will take two years to heal.

My daughter begs to swim with me, to bike with me, to go down the slide with me at the park. I try to keep up like I used to, but the fetus presses against my diaphragm, and my loosening ligaments cause my hips to click as I walk.

I begin to research unintended pregnancies. In tabs I hide from my husband but keep on my browser for months, I discover how unoriginal I am. Just shy of half the pregnancies in the United States are unintended, the Guttmacher Institute and Centers for Disease Control and Prevention report, and many of those women are using birth control. In 2008, 1,272,000 women became pregnant after missing a pill or "incorrectly using a barrier method during some acts of intercourse," while 155,000 women became pregnant after using contraception perfectly.

I fall into the first category. I had hated hormonal birth control—the mood swings and weight gain and risk of deadly blood clots—so I didn't go back on it after the birth of my daughter.

Instead, I wanted to let my body be my body, unmanipulated and free, and we used nonhormonal means. Though at some point, we must have done something wrong. Or *I* did something wrong. When discussing contraception, the Guttmacher Institute only uses the term "women." It assumes the responsibility rests primarily on females; it never references "contraceptives" and "men."

In early November, an external safety review stops testing on a hormonal, two-injection birth control for men. The reason: too many men dropped out of the study due to acne, mood swings, and depression.

Around the same time, *JAMA Psychiatry* publishes a Dutch study that links depression to hormonal birth control in women. The "use of hormonal contraception," the study reports, "was associated with subsequent use of antidepressants and a first diagnosis of depression, suggesting depression as a potential adverse effect of hormonal contraceptive." Though women have long said hormonal birth control can lead to depression—and though some women have tried out multiple forms of birth control before discovering the correct hormonal cocktail for their bodies—this is the first study to suggest the link's truth.

Feminist groups discuss both studies as a sign of institutional sexism, yet the pushback is immediate. NPR science correspondent Rob Stein says there's "a different risk-benefit analysis when it comes to men using a contraceptive. When women use a contraceptive, they're balancing the risks of the drug against the risks of getting pregnant. And pregnancy itself carries risks. But these are healthy men—they're not going to suffer any risks if they get somebody else pregnant."

Jeffrey Jensen of the Women's Health Research Unit at Oregon Health and Science University similarly downplays the *JAMA* study: "Depression is common. Contraception use is common. So both of those things are commonly going to occur together."

"It's a tragedy of the riches," he goes on to say. "If you really want to be depressed, have an unintended pregnancy."

On the last point, at least, Jensen is right. I schedule ob-gyn appointments and take prenatal vitamins, but after I drop my daughter off at preschool, I also willfully imagine myself getting hit by a truck. Day after day, I pause near the roundabout. Day after day, trucks hurtle toward me. As my belly bloats against my seatbelt, I think, *It's okay if I die. It's okay if it hits me. If I sped out right now, it would smash into my door. It wouldn't really matter. I've made a mistake I can't get out of. I've already ruined the life of this child.*

I get counseling and try to think positively about the birth, but a journal entry of mine, written in early November, is full of fear. Fear that I won't bond. That I won't be happy. That something will go very, very wrong, and I won't be a good mother to my child.

On Tuesday, November 8, the day of the 2016 election, I am thirty-six weeks pregnant. The infant I am carrying butts his head against my pubic bone, swelling my perineum. I cannot get out of bed or the car without a sharp pain in my hip, and my abdomen is so large and immobile I bump into doorknobs and burn my stomach on the stove. When I have a Braxton-Hicks contraction, my watermelon-sized uterus suddenly hardens into stone and I cannot breathe. At night, I wake up on my back, stiff, as if suffocating.

The sensation does not diminish when I turn on the news.

Three weeks later, I am bleeding. My son comes so quick, I drench our bedroom carpet with amniotic fluid, and the placenta lands in a bloody blob on the bathroom floor. Our son is healthy. Alive. I am healthy and alive, too, though I require two inches of stitches, and for four weeks I must spray myself with a peri bottle every time I use the bathroom.

"You could see there was blood coming out of her eyes. Blood coming out of her wherever."

—Donald Trump

In the hazy weeks that follow, the margin in the popular vote widens. Hillary Clinton leads Trump by nearly 3 million votes. Articles are published about the Electoral College and what loopholes the constitution allows for such results. Liberals and conservatives opposed to Trump call their state's electors, imploring them to vote for Clinton instead. But on December 19, the results do not change.

On December 19, I am home alone with both children for the first time and on the verge of tears for no clear reason other than the fact that they are demanding all of my time. Someone always needs something—breast milk, a snack, a diaper change, a Band-Aid, a hug. I spend the day with one hand lifting my shirt for my son, the other reaching for my daughter.

I feel pessimistic. I fear military action. I fear a quickening of environmental destruction that we won't be able to recover from. As my son's jaw moves up and down and he takes long gulps, I think, *What will the future be like for this child?* The walls close in on me. I want to speak out, like my colleagues and friends who are making dozens of phone calls a week and writing long editorials, but my writing is fragmented and I can't get more than ten minutes alone.

I make plans to attend the Arkansas Women's March. My husband asks if I'm sure I'll be safe. My mother-in-law asks why some marches aren't welcoming pro-life organizations. My mother-in-law was in college in the 1970s. She said she was pro-choice, but she says her opinions changed after she had children. "Life begins at conception. We know this now," she tells me.

Many of my extended family members are pro-life. When I borrowed my grandmother's car for a week in college, I peeled her "Abortion Stops a Beating Heart" window cling from the back seat. It wasn't that I advocated abortions—on the morality of the procedure, I, then a liberal Catholic, was confused—but I believed they were a deeply personal choice, and not a choice I or anyone else could dictate or judge. When I returned the car at the end of the week, I forgot to put the cling back up. My grandma stared at the empty spot, looked at me, and frowned.

When I was pregnant with my first child, my utter amazement at the experience of being pregnant made me, too, reconsider abortions. *How,* I wondered, my hand to my belly, *could anyone not be overwhelmed with this awe?*

When I was pregnant with my second, I felt erased. Swallowed whole. I sensed myself staring at a dark path, and I knew the version of myself that came out of it would not be the version of myself going in.

At the Arkansas Women's March, I wear my son in a wrap. He breastfeeds during the speeches, which I find humorously appropriate. *A young feminist*, my friends and I tease. An older woman comes up to me, despair pulling her face. She says she's marching for her grandchildren.

I feel empowered. Caught up. I am heartened to see the crowd, though I get an odd catch in my throat when I cradle my son and remember all the nights I curled in on myself, silenced by the ever-growing weight of the child.

When the crowds at the women's marches far exceed those from his inauguration, Trump critiques the entertainment and asks, "Why didn't these people vote?"

Shortly after, Trump signs one of his first executive orders and rescinds funding from any NGO that even refers a woman to another organization for an abortion. The publicity photograph shows Trump at his desk, surrounded by seven other white men.

Though I recognize that I love and am bonding with my son, the thought of other women staring down that same dark path fills me with horror. After we've put the kids to bed, I argue with my husband about politics, demand to know why he isn't as angry as me, and slam the bedroom door.

I return to work. I adjust my life to a new routine: waking in the dark to the sound of my husband leaving, getting both children up, feeding my daughter, changing and nursing my son, getting myself in the shower, hoping my son's either still sleeping or happy in the bouncer in the bathroom while I, myself, get

dressed and fed. Gathering material, including the bottles from
the fridge, a smaller cooler with fresh ice packs, and all the parts
of my breast pump. My daughter's preschool takes attendance. In
that first month alone, we are tardy five times.

After work, I pick my children up, my husband returns from
work, we make dinner, we eat dinner, and I nurse my son at least
two times, though in those first few weeks he's still cluster feeding every thirty to forty minutes. I stand, exhausted, at the sink
in the evening, the pump parts floating in hot water: the rubbery
valves, the flanges, the collection containers, the bottles, the nipples. I wash and rinse them while my husband helps my daughter
brush her teeth, and it seems that all of life has become these
small tasks. My back aches. I want to lie down. Instead, I dip my
hand into the water and pull out another valve.

In February, the GOP launches its health care reform. It wants
to repeal and replace the Affordable Care Act, though what the
repeal will look like has not taken shape. The Affordable Care
Act that ensures access to birth control and maternity care, and
obliges employers to provide a clean, private space for working
mothers to pump, and requires insurance companies to cover
breast pumps so that all mothers, if they want to breastfeed while
working full time, can access the equipment they need.

At work, I pump breast milk three times a day. I close my door
and listen to the motor. I know others can hear it, whether in
the hallway or the offices beside me. Sometimes students or colleagues knock on my door while I am pumping, and I have to
suppress a sudden panic. "Just a minute," I say. I am sitting at my
desk, my shirt lifted, my nipples caught in the suction of the two
flanges.

When colleagues ask how I am adjusting, I do not know how to respond. I want to be at work, and yet when I kiss my son, he smells so much like his day care I almost cry.

I forget the bottles at home and have to rush to retrieve them between two classes. I get stuck behind a train and am almost late.

I feel the full effects and costs of early motherhood—the sleep deprivation, the hormonal shifts, the $25,000-plus average spent in an infant's first two years—as funding for Planned Parenthood is being repealed and newspaper articles announce that Trump's cabinet is the whitest and most patriarchal since Reagan.

I remain haunted.

Midway through my pregnancy, a few weeks before we found out the sex, I dreamt I gave birth to a boy. In the dream, I was disappointed. A film formed between us, a dark scrim. I pushed the baby away and did not bond with the child.

When I mentioned the dream to the counselor I was seeing for prenatal depression, she brushed aside my fear that the dream would come true and instead asked, "What men in your life are you mad at?"

That spring, Oklahoma state representative Justin Humphrey calls pregnant women "hosts." He proposes a bill that requires women to get permission from the fetus's father to have an abortion. "I understand that they [women] feel like that is their body. I feel like it is a separate—what I call them is, is you're a 'host.' And you know when you enter into a relationship you're going to be that host and so ... after you're irresponsible then don't claim, well, I can just go and do this with another body, when you're the host and you invited that in."

In my home state of Arkansas, ranked fourth worst for women's representation in the government, new legislation bans the safest form of second trimester abortions. New legislation requires any doctor providing an abortion to first obtain a full medical history of previous pregnancies. The second bill is intended as a roadblock, even though Arkansas only has one clinical abortion provider and patients must make two visits, forty-eight hours apart.

Arkansas also passes a law allowing men to stop women from having an abortion. According to the new bill, the biological father can step in and say no. There is no clause excluding rapists from being considered biological fathers.

In March, my son catches respiratory syncytial virus. He coughs and wheezes like an eighty-year-old smoker, even though his lungs, together, are the size of my single fist. I bring him to the pediatrician's office three times in a single week. They take an x-ray of his lungs and inject steroids into his chunky thigh.

I am tired. We are not sleeping well. I stop watching the news because it depresses me and I am already feeling drained and depressed. By the end of the week, when I stand on the scale at home, I discover I'm back down to my prepregnancy weight— seven months quicker than it took with my daughter. I can feel the hard curve of my hip bone again, and the pants that were snug a year ago sag even when tied.

On the prenatal/postpartum depression forums I occasionally visit, women who suffered terribly after their first child sometimes post about second pregnancies—some unintended, some not. They are terrified about experiencing postpartum depression again. "I am so lonely," one of the women writes.

My family and I sit on the couch. My son is nursing. My daughter rubs a mole on my side.
Entirely surrounded by children's skin, I almost can't breathe.
"I love you all," my husband says. Then, he leans over and whispers in my ear, "but I love you the most."

From Roxane Gay's *Bad Feminist*, which I read on the couch while nursing my son: "Since 1973, women in the United States have had the right to choose to terminate a pregnancy. Women have had the right to choose not to be forced into unwanted motherhood."

To be forced into unwanted motherhood. The words catch me. Did I feel forced?
At the dinner table, my son cries from hunger. While my daughter and husband interrupt each other to talk about their days, I breastfeed on one side and then the other, eating awkwardly with my nondominant hand. Any energy I have drains from me into him.
"You realize I did this for us. I did this for you," I tell my husband.

Later that evening, I sit alone in the car in a parking lot. It is raining. I wonder how long things can continue before I lose grip of who I am. In a nightmarish kind of way, it feels all too possible: that I have sacrificed too much, stepped over a line that protects my own sanity, and that I one day might pack a bag and run away.

"Are you going to run away?" my mother had asked me a few
weeks after the birth. I had looked at her, startled. What in my
face made that a question she thought she should ask?

On Mother's Day, the local church that covered its lawn with
Trump placards in the fall has a new sign:

EVE WASN'T A PERFECT MOM

BUT GOD STILL FORGAVE HER.

We drive by the church on the way to a park, where we eat a
picnic lunch and wade in the lake. Across the beach, a minister
baptizes adults in murky water.

My husband and I grew up Catholic. We were married in a
Catholic church. On my first Mother's Day after the birth of
my daughter, the church we occasionally attended handed out
magnets: "Mothers are the heart of the family."

Oklahoma state representative Justin Humphrey considers
women hosts.
    Divine hosts? I begin to think. *Parasitic hosts?*
    Is there a difference?

In early May, the House of Representatives passes their second
attempt to replace and repeal the Affordable Care Act. This new
bill will allow states to consider pregnancy a preexisting condition, thus allowing pregnant women to be placed in high-risk
insurance pools. Estimates suggest that women of child-rearing
age who want maternity coverage will pay $1,000 more a month
than men of the same age. Neither the meeting the White House

organizes with House representatives nor the Senate's review committee includes any women.

The next morning, my daughter joins me in the shower. She slips off her spacesuit pajamas, her rainbow underwear, and insists, at age four, that she's old enough to graduate from the bath. Her body is thin, her stomach the smooth and rounded stomach of a child, unlike my own, still puckered and pocked from the birth of my son.

I rub the luffa over her back and then my own. I scrub between my breasts. My daughter, hunched forward, wraps an arm around my thigh.

When I press my forehead into the tile, I want to destroy either myself or these walls.

"Why wouldn't you let us discuss the possibility of an abortion?" I ask my husband.

It's odd timing, I know. Our son is here. He coos and rolls over and has started to laugh, though it's a laugh unlike any other I have heard. A throaty caw that makes me giggle. But I need to ask. And I need to know.

My husband hesitates. "Because it's my child, too, and I feel responsible. I want to take care of him."

My husband, I know, is genuine. He considers himself responsible. Following through with the pregnancy was never a question for him.

And yet, in his response, something nags at me: the assumption—the honorable assumption, yes, but the assumption, just the same—that he has an equal say. Or more: that his desire to have an equal say, and to take responsibility for our unintended pregnancy, overwhelmed my own ability to make a decision about my body.

In the weeks before I gave birth to my daughter, when my husband and I spent evenings curled next to each other, his hands on my belly, he said that if something went wrong, he'd rather lose the baby than me. He loved me, and I was the known quantity. The infant was not.

It was a touching moment. I understood it. And if it came between choosing one life over another—mine over the fetus's—I'd understand that difficult, difficult choice.

Yet death isn't the only way to lose a life. Did I have the choice to say I wanted to choose my own wellbeing over that of an unintended fetus? Are my choices in this culture so firmly dictated by my ability to give birth?

Growing up, I sometimes wished I wasn't female. I did not want to be male, but I didn't want to be female. How could I feel empowered when our culture places so many of the costs, and risks, and burdens of sexual reproduction on women?

A pro-life meme that circulates around Mother's Day:

NOT A MISTAKE.

NOT A BURDEN.

NOT A PROBLEM.

NOT A PUNISHMENT.

NOT AN INCONVENIENCE.

NOT A NUISANCE.

NOT AN ACCIDENT.

A MIRACLE.

In the evening, just after I've swaddled my son and laid him down in the crib, I ask my husband again why he wouldn't let us even discuss an abortion. My husband grows silent. He clenches his jaw. His left foot begins to shake on the coffee table where he's propped it. "I just can't…it's not moral…," he says, and I almost begin to cry, because I can see his suffering—the wrenching of his chest as he turns away from me.

"Even knowing what it did to me? Even knowing how miserable I was?" I say, almost pleading. Then, softer, "If I had had an abortion, would our marriage have ended?"

His answer is a whisper. "I don't know. Maybe."

What I want him to say: "You are important. Your body is important. What decisions you make about your body are important, and you are not beholden to anyone else when making those decisions. I never should have placed you in that position. I should have told you I'd support and respect any decision you made. I am sorry."

Instead, he can't let go of the fact that some of that decision should have been his, too. That he needed a say. The fact that it was my body—and that I would bear most of the burdens in those first two years—didn't make it more of my own choice.

What I want is exactly what he can't give.

We sit on the couch, three and a half years of the Trump administration ahead of us, and it doesn't matter just now what reconciliation we'll come to. My bra smells of breast milk. Our son, whom we both love, cries in the bedroom. Like the country around us, we are cutting new teeth.

BIRTH (UN)MEDICALIZED

A CASE STUDY

ABSTRACT

Hospitals are accustomed to ordering chaos—the lacerated, broken, gaping trauma patient is wheeled into the ER, where staff swiftly open the airway, stop the bleeding, and set the bone. They stabilize. Childbirth, on the other hand, is chaos that the body can resolve itself. If everything goes normally, order will come—a baby will be born, creation will trump destruction. The birth attendant can help support the maternal body's own resolution, or the birth attendant can manage and control the process with modern means. Support versus stabilize. In the vast majority of US hospitals today, birth is stabilized.

—Jennifer Block, *Pushed: The Painful Truth about Childbirth and Modern Maternity Care*

INTRODUCTION

A few weeks after we discover I am pregnant with our second child, my husband and I sit down to discuss which practitioner to use for the birth. The pregnancy books we studied four years earlier lay on the coffee table in front of us—a familiar sight—and yet we hesitate and halt just as we had the first time around. In eight months, we will have a second child. The time period warps before us, both incredibly long and incredibly short, and on the couch of our rented duplex, baby items stuffed in our daughter's closet, the decision seems crucial. Damning.

When I was pregnant with our first child, I read obsessively about birth choices, mining online forums and the basement stacks of the library for any information I could get. The choices at times overwhelmed me, but I was the kind of person who hated the fog of Benadryl and doctor offices, so I decided to work with a midwife—a woman who put me at ease until my blood pressure spiked and an induction left me flat on my back, hooked up to an IV, laboring mostly in a hospital bed.

This time around, I vow I will do everything I can to have a more empowering birth experience. However, between pregnancies I have taken a job in Arkansas. Unlike New York, Arkansas does not allow nurse midwives to practice in hospitals, so I am left with two extremes: (1) Use an ob-gyn and give birth in the hospital—the system our health insurance is built to cover. (2) Use a licensed lay midwife and give birth at home—which our health insurance will only cover after the fact, requiring us to pay the midwife up front.

We do not have four thousand dollars in the bank. We do not have room in our rented duplex for a water birth's inflatable pool. We do not, even, have a quiet, secluded space in our duplex where my daughter won't hear me. Yet a midwife will know my name whereas an OB will likely have to look at a chart, so I lean toward her just the same.

Nonetheless, when I mention the term "home birth," my husband prickles, jumps, and turns skittish. "What if your blood pressure goes up again?" he asks. "What if you need medical attention and we can't get to the hospital fast enough?" He reminds me of the high blood pressure numbers I had with my daughter, the oxygen mask the nurses placed over my mouth during the last stages of her birth, and the nurse's concern that I might be hemorrhaging. He reminds me of our daughter in the special care nursery—her tiny head hidden beneath an oxygen hood. He envisions emergency: blood on the floor, panic, a tiny body, and somebody's death.

Sitting there, newly pregnant, I want to believe that my body is capable of getting through birth without medical intervention. I want to believe that I will be fine, and my body won't turn against me. But I also suddenly recall the high blood pressure with my daughter; the sense that something very wrong could be, and perhaps was, happening. That birth is a risk, and that I might not come out of it unscathed. *Maybe my body can't do it*, I begin to think. *Maybe it would be better to have medical support close by.*

HYPOTHESIS

The question I am asking is about the medicalization of women's bodies, but I cannot answer it without first addressing fear. The kind of fear my husband and I base our decision on: that childbirth is dangerous, and that it places the mother at risk and must be carefully monitored.

Some of these fears, of course, are warranted. Women and fetuses do die during pregnancy and birth. I know a woman whose placenta suddenly detached from her uterus, killing the fetus just weeks before the due date, and a friend of mine had emergency surgery after an ectopic pregnancy caused her fallopian tube to burst. My own midwife induced me for high blood pressure because it is the first symptom of preeclampsia, a condition that will kill the mother unless she quickly delivers the infant. Physicians have responded to all of these concerns by carefully monitoring pregnant women and doing what they need to keep the child healthy. Practitioners swoop in and conduct an emergency C-section sooner than they sometimes need to in the fear that, if something goes wrong, someone will die and they may be sued. But I also can't help but wonder what it means when women and partners and practitioners alike respond out of fear—fear of the infant or mother's death. Especially when 99.9 percent of women will survive childbirth, and 99.4 percent of infants will survive their first year.

Fear, the well-renowned midwife Ina May Gaskin says, slows labor. In her *Guide to Childbirth*, Gaskin spends a significant amount of time describing sphincter muscles—excretory, cervical, and vaginal. All work best when relaxed. When someone experiences fear—or if they feel self-conscious and vulnerable—adrenaline prevents the sphincter muscles from releasing. Because most women fear physical pain and have been taught to fear childbirth—and because most hospital settings do not offer privacy—women have trouble relaxing, which causes the cervix to tighten and stop dilating, rather than to open and soften. In a culture of fear, Gaskin concludes that a woman's chance of having a successful, natural birth are sabotaged from the start.

Pregnant a second time and envisioning the upcoming birth, what I feel is, indeed, fear. I can sense myself pulling inward and clenching, my arms wrapped tight around my growing belly. I do not want statistics and the beeping of a hospital monitor to overwhelm my wishes, my body, and my very *self*. I do not want to lose my autonomy and be objectified and pathologized, looked at as a number, or a series of numbers: centimeters dilated, blood pressure rising. I simply want to be seen as a woman experiencing birth. I want the people around me to respect me, and, in moments of self-questioning and doubt, I want the people around me to help me respect myself.

In *Brought to Bed*, which I read halfway through my pregnancy, Judith Walzer Leavitt traces the cultural forces that moved births from the home, where women were tended by female midwives and female neighbors, to the hospital, where they were treated by male physicians. Most American women in the nineteenth century advocated for this change. They'd been taught to fear childbirth, and they—like many women today—desired the reprieve of medication. Yet the transition from home births to hospital births, where women could receive these drugs, placed birth under the control of a medical institution that had long defined women as the weaker and often invalid sex. As Leavitt describes, many physicians and medical students found the subject of childbirth so "embarrassing" that they averted their eyes during any live demonstrations and generally relied instead on a "theoretical education." They trusted books written by men and observations made by men rather than the bodies bearing down before them.

Even more, when obstetricians began taking over birth, the male physicians disregarded centuries of midwifery practices and laboring positions—kneeling, hands and knees, squatting—and had women deliver flat on their backs, which allowed men a better view of the cervix and more access to the birth canal. However, the position forced women to push against gravity and thus caused more difficult deliveries and an increase in episiotomies and tears. Today, even though we know better, most women in hospitals continue to give birth in the lithotomy position: stirrups and all.

Also troubling: most women in the first half of the twentieth century weren't even alert for the birth of their children. They went to a hospital, received a combination of scopolamine and morphine, and promptly lost consciousness. As they drifted through their drug-induced dreamscape, their bodies thrashed so violently that hospitals began to tether the women's arms and legs to their beds. Some hospitals even began confining unconscious, laboring women in a "crib-bed"—a sort of inescapable cage created from thick sheets. The women would wake hours or days later, without any memories of the birth but bruised at their wrists, their vaginas and perinea swollen and torn from forceps.

It wasn't until the late 1950s that women began to question twilight sleep. This is when the natural childbirth movement began to blossom and grow—and when Ida May Gaskin began to practice. But obstetrics had already engrained itself so thoroughly in the US medical system that natural birth struggled to establish itself as an equal alternative. In addition, the invention of plastics led to the spinal block and later the epidural, and even though epidurals routinely led to a drop in blood pressure, requiring Pitocin to speed up labor again, and even though both drugs, combined, limit women to the hospital bed and can cause breathing issues in the infant, and even though all of these things have led to increased injuries of the pelvic floor (problems women today continue to deal with, often silently and with shame), the realities of these interventions remain underrecognized. "Think about the side effects," an RN warns my hospital's childbirth class, knowing, nonetheless, that most of us will have an intervention. Interventions and epidurals are the norm. Hospital births are built around them.

Perhaps most concerning: when a woman enters a hospital to give birth, she in many ways gives up the rights to her body. The women I talk to cringe at the thought of an episiotomy. They would each rather their perineum tears than be cut by a doctor. Yet I read about women whose perinea are cut just the same when crowning infants stretch their skin to the doctors' limit.

I also talk to and read about women who can't find a practitioner willing to let them attempt a vaginal birth after a previous C-section. Citing the 0.5 to 1.5 percent chance that a VBAC, as it is called, might cause a rupture and require emergency surgery, the doctors or hospitals refuse altogether. This, of course, ignores the fact that US hospitals have a 32 percent C-section rate, when the World Health Organization recommends a C-section rate between 10 and 15 percent, and that many emergency C-sections are not actually emergencies but rather attempts to speed up the process. "Your Biggest C-Section Risk May Be Your Hospital," the title of a *Consumer Reports* article reads. Some women who desire a VBAC end up giving birth at home, unassisted, because they can't find a practitioner. A few women have been arrested. Other women are simply forced to undergo a second surgery.

I pause here, confused. Having grown up in an era that believed feminism had given women the "right to choose," I find myself perplexed and uncomfortable with the constraints placed on pregnant bodies. Feminism has fought for women's access to various types of birth control, including abortion, and the right for women to live lives separate from motherhood, and yet the moment a woman wants to become or becomes a mother—no matter her stance on feminism or abortion—she suddenly loses the ability to decide how and with whom she wants to give birth. Instead, the medical industry takes over, shuttling her through a system that promotes certain interventions while dictating where the delivery should take place.

"Women's autonomy means both the right to legal abortion and the right to a vaginal birth after cesarean—you can't have one without the other," Jennifer Block writes in *Pushed*. And yet her response—like that of so many others who advocate for better birth practices—is to call on women to research and make informed decisions about practitioners, pain medication, and interventions. When I think back to both of my pregnancies—all those times I sat on the couch, leafing through booklets and pamphlets, trying to communicate to my husband and myself things I did not yet know how to say—I bristle, slightly, as the onus of change is placed back on me.

It seems ludicrous to me that within nine months—even less than that, really—a woman is expected to unravel the entire history of childbirth in the West. To dig into statistics that are hidden. To analyze cultural motives at play in C-sections. To interrogate society's expectations for childbirth and to separate those societal expectations from what she knows is best for her. All while her body morphs and transforms at speeds she has never experienced before. Who wouldn't be overwhelmed?

This, I begin to think, is how systems of oppression continue. The oppressed don't have the full story. They do not have time to get the whole story. Nine months go by, and the woman gives birth whether she wants to or not, in the way she wants to or not, according to her birth plan or not, and then she is left to live with the story, and the story is in the past—something she cannot change.

METHODS

PARTICIPANTS AND PROCEDURES

My body continues to change, my uterus expanding, my hips widening, and despite my hesitations, I work with an ob-gyn. She is nice enough, but the appointments are impersonal. I often spend thirty to forty minutes past my appointment time

in the waiting area, quietly scrolling through my phone or eyeing the other women who come in and out of the office. The
television runs through health advertisements about osteoporosis and prenatal exercise. A cabinet holds a small fridge with
water and a basket with granola bars and fruit snacks. When
the nurse finally calls me, I pee in a plastic cup, which I label
with my name and slide through the metal pass-through to the
laboratory. The nurse weighs me and takes my blood pressure.
Then I spend another ten to thirty minutes in the exam room,
sometimes with a paper sheet wrapped around my waist, my
underwear stuffed between my pants, which I have folded and
placed on the single plastic chair in the corner. It seems I am
always waiting. Waiting and waiting. Finally, my doctor comes
in, and though she is a female, supposedly receptive to unmedicated births, she is quick and brief. Unless I ask a question
right away, she does not engage with me past the polite façade
I provide. I spend more than an hour in the ob-gyn clinic, but
my face time with the doctor lasts less than five minutes. *Your
numbers look fine*, she tells me. *The baby is growing as he should. I'll
see you in two weeks.* I schedule another appointment and check
out. My movements are slow. Methodical. I squint into the sun
when I exit the building. I do not feel fully seen, fully heard, and
so I hire a doula.

Prior to my second pregnancy, I'd hardly heard the term
"doula," let alone considered hiring one. I had probably considered a doula a bit excessive. Paying for a woman to talk to me
about pregnancy, rub my back during labor, and suggest positions
for delivery? I considered such an arrangement appropriate for
wealthy women who wanted to be coddled throughout their
pregnancies. Not me. But Arkansas, perhaps because of its limited birth options, sustains plenty of doulas, and the doula as a

result offered a kind of middle ground between a hospital birth and a home birth.

That said, the doula is not exactly an ideal compromise. In *Pushed*, Block chronicles the recent rise of doulas, calling them a "vestige" of the female labor support system that existed prior to the movement to hospitals. Her reasoning: when most women still gave birth at home, female neighbors and family members routinely aided the birthing mother by completing household tasks, tending other children, and supporting her physically and emotionally during delivery. The practice was communal. Women simply helped each other, knowing they'd receive the same help in turn.

We have since lost this social birth. As Block ironically states, women in the twentieth century experiencing twilight sleep didn't need labor support when they were unconscious. But as we've shifted into different birthing practices, the doula has re-emerged to remind us of the physical and emotional needs of the mother. In many ways, Block writes, doulas today represent a lack of faith in the current medical industry. Would I hire a doula if I knew I'd be cared for in a hospital setting? No. Of course not.

Cultural history aside, it doesn't escape me that I pay for my doula. One thousand dollars, to be exact. It isn't a small sum of money, especially when added to other birthing costs, and the fact that I can afford it says something about privilege. I am going out of my way to appropriate physical and emotional support for labor, and by paying for that support, I am supporting a consumer industry that withholds that support from women with less disposable income than me.

It troubles me, and I flinch a little as I write a check for each two-hundred-dollar installment. Nonetheless, my determination to have a natural birth—or at least as close to a natural birth as

possible—makes the idea of feeling cared for through my pregnancy and delivery too appealing to refuse. My doula will support
my birth plan. She will come to my house during labor and help
me decide when to go to the hospital. She will suggest positions
for labor and delivery and massage my shoulders or back if that's
what I need. She also offers prenatal visits. Every month for an
hour, I sit on a birth ball in her office, bouncing up and down as
we discuss my mood, my symptoms, and what I can do to relieve
those symptoms. She shows me how to use the couch to get into
an inversion that will flip the baby. She shows me squats and
exercises I can do to guide the baby into the optimal position.
We talk about my diet, how much water I am drinking, and how
to get enough exercise in Arkansas's hot summers. Unlike my
ob-gyn, she knows of the anxiety I begin to feel near the end of
the pregnancy and my concern that I won't have enough support
after the birth.

In working with her, I feel hope rather than fear, and I am
heartened by her encouragement: that I can have a positive birth
experience, and that I can be empowered.

POTENTIAL LIMITATIONS

One afternoon during the third trimester of my second pregnancy, when I can no longer climb a flight of stairs without
losing my breath, I open a social media site and discover Sarah
Blackwood's essay "Monstrous Births." Citing her own difficult
births, each of which resulted in a C-section, Blackwood writes,
"Religious dogma once saw childbirth as punishment, 'natural'
birth proponents see it as empowering," and both are equally
damaging. She calls on society to recognize birth as "grisly,
frightening, and astonishing" rather than right or wrong, correct
or incorrect, or symbolic of strength or weakness. In particular,

she warns against the latter, which she equates with feminism's
tales of strength. "I prefer to hear, tell, and read stories about
childbirth that give the lie to contemporary fantasies about empowerment," she concludes. "Birth is a monstrous thing, and it
has no moral component."

Although Blackwood's valorization of the "monstrous" (and
critique of empowerment) seems to create its own dichotomy,
my heart rate nonetheless quickens as I read, and I press one
hand to my belly, against my son's kicks. I have begun to second
guess my choice of practitioners—to wish I'd gone with the midwife after all—but as I read through the substantial, somewhat
polarizing comments that follow Blackwood's essay, I suddenly
reconsider my line of thinking. Is my desire for a natural childbirth purely ideological? Have I been pulled in by the rhetoric
of the natural birth movement and my own white, middle-class
granola-ism, to believe that experiencing a natural birth will lead
to empowerment?

It's a difficult question. Yet, reading Blackwood's story and
the stories other women share in response, I am struck again
and again by how quickly women move to defend their choices.
Women who had planned C-sections protect themselves from
the critique that planned C-sections are unhealthy, and that they
aren't "real" women because they didn't give birth naturally. Those
who had unplanned C-sections (including Blackwood) guard
themselves from the accusation that their body failed them or
that they gave in too early. Those who have unmedicated births
also fall victim to insecurity. They protect themselves from
Blackwood's argument that they are buying into a faulty belief
that unmedicated births are better or more empowering than
other forms of birth.

Stepping back, what strikes me the most about all this

judgment is how it works to obscure the system. Women are judging themselves and others—striving to have the "ideal" birth—and in doing so, they are spending so much energy scrutinizing everyone's choices that they overlook the cultural systems that are encouraging them to criticize and condemn others in the first place. Cultural systems that put the weight of a certain type of birth on the mother's shoulders rather than calling on society as a whole to interrogate itself and realize how much its own components—the medical institutions, the stories we tell about birth, and even the insurance companies—limit women's choices and make the way they give birth seem like it has so much at stake.

I am similarly saddened by how many women—including Blackwood—struggle with their birth stories and wish something had happened differently. And more and more, I expect that something *should*, indeed, have happened differently. I think back to Gaskin's insistence that birth can be positive and safe if we learn to approach the process with respect rather than fear. Yet is that even possible in our society? How can a woman be vulnerable, let go of her conscious self and give control to her body—letting it do the work it needs to do—when she knows how much she might be judged, when she is scared, and when the culture, as a whole, has not been kind to vulnerable women?

As my due date nears, and I become more and more uncomfortable, and my feet begin to swell—the tops puffy even in the morning, and the Braxton-Hicks contractions nearly constant, but not yet in a pattern—I wonder what the birth will be like. I tell myself to trust my body. It becomes a mantra. And yet beneath that brews fear and anxiety—that maybe all my research is wrong. Maybe I simply can't do it. Maybe my birth experience will show me something others have known all along: that I am ill-equipped, and that without a watchful eye, childbirth will kill me.

RESULTS

My birth begins at 3 a.m. when I wake with a rock-hard uterus that softens and then hardens again. I have been waking with such Braxton-Hicks contractions for days, at exactly this time, so at first I do not think anything about them. I drink a glass of milk, get back into bed, and then, when they continue, decide to take a bath, which has stopped stubborn Braxton-Hicks contractions in the past. I fill the tub with warm water and keep the light off. My daughter sleeps across the house. My husband snores from the other room. I ease myself in, my belly so large that it pokes out of the water like an island. The contractions tighten, and I breathe in and out, cringing sometimes from their strength. I cannot get comfortable in the tub. All is silent, and my silent discomfort encloses me. I listen to the static of the house, the house and the water a strange cocoon, neither comforting nor unsettling.

When the contractions do not abate, I get out. I dry myself and walk into the kitchen, the contractions still coming, not constant but stronger. Sometimes I grab the counter, arching my back and leaning in. I keep eyeing the clock, timing them. Five minutes apart. Then ten. Then two, then five, then nine again. Unnerving. Frustrating. I walk around the house. The contractions begin to burn, a deep ember filling my back and belly. I can't think of anything during them, but I reach for a wall. "Is this it?" I wonder. I want to be sure, but I am not sure. It is only when they overtake me that I realize something is coming that I cannot stop.

At 5:30 I wake my husband. "I think I'm in labor," I say, a hand on my aching, burning belly, my lower back aflame. They've suddenly found their pattern—five minutes apart, maybe shorter. I've stopped looking at the clock and have just begun to breathe.

The next thirty or so minutes are a strange film. My husband gets out of bed. "Okay. I'll take a quick shower."

"You don't have time for a shower," I say, knowing, somehow, that this is urgent. My husband calls the doula. He calls the friend who's said she'll watch our daughter. He scrambles around the house in his underwear, packing the last of the items in our hospital bag. The contractions come quicker. He calls the doula again.

"How long apart are they?" she asks.

"They were five," I say. "Now it's three. Maybe two," and it is true. I am on my hands and knees in the bedroom, arching my back. I crawl toward the bed and kneel. I bite into the edge of the mattress. I clench the mattress and the blankets during the contractions. I tell myself to relax, like Gaskin wrote, though during the peak of the contractions I bite and press into the bed with a force that surprises me. I moan. I hardly made a noise during the birth of my daughter, but this time I cannot help it. I moan into the bed, into the night. My doula hears my moans on the phone, and tells me later that from the sound she knew I had already passed through the early and mid stages of labor.

"We need to get to the hospital," I say, almost pleading, though in between contractions I am thinking of my daughter. My friend is still a half hour away and I don't want my daughter in the car with us, in the hospital with us, aware of my pain. I imagine her in the fluorescent lights of the waiting room, confused and scared. In short sentences, I tell my husband to call another friend who lives closer. He begins to panic, still in his underwear, still scrambling around. "I need help," I say, as another contraction comes on, and I realize, I know, moaning again into the bed, that I am alone in this. Despite my carefully laid plans, despite my husband's presence, no one is here for me. But the sensations are familiar, and I recognize that, too. I feel a pressure in my perineum that I recall from the birth of my daughter. "He's coming," I say. "Now."

The contractions wrap around my belly, and I moan into the bed as a force pushes down. I feel the force of it meet resistance from bone, from pelvis, and my water breaks, drenching my legs and the floor. "He's coming," I say again, and I can sense the panic in my husband, my doula by now on speaker phone, talking to him, to us, though I am no longer paying attention. Two, maybe three more contractions, a push that I cannot stop. I feel the pressure, the something emerging, receding back in. I slip one leg out of my pants, and then the something emerging is fully emerging, and my husband kneels behind me, guiding the baby, more slippery than he expects, from my body to the floor.

I turn, and there my son is: still connected to me by umbilical cord, a whitish being, scrunched, wrinkled, with white goop and red streaks, miraculously alive in the world.

I scoop him up. I crawl into the bathroom, where I squat as the afterbirth slips from me. We debate what to do next—whether to try and drive to the hospital ourselves or call an ambulance—but despite the alarm I register on my husband's face, I do not feel rushed or panicked. On the contrary, I feel completely fine.

DISCUSSION

This is the part I cling to, now: I was fine. It was not the birth experience I expected. (When is anything what we expect?) It was not the birth experience I could have planned for. But I did it, and I did it without medication or interventions. In the seclusion of our home, I had the experience I had sought.

Yet I have to fight for that story once others hear about my

son's birth. "You must have been so scared!" people say—everyone
from the friends who text me or ask for the story over coffee, to
the nurses at the hospital, which we went to later that morning.
My father-in-law, in his Christmas letter that year, describes how
"things reached a critical moment." A colleague tells me, "I heard
it was an unideal situation."

For a while, even my husband uses such terms. Those first few
days, whenever I insist that everything went well, my husband
grimaces. His own memories of panic, his own sense of a loss of
control, and his own fear that our son wasn't crying loud enough
overwhelm him. It will take weeks for him to soften to the experience of our accidental home birth and begin to recount his own
story not with fear, but with pride.

All of their words flummox and aggravate me. My son's birth
was not an emergency. It was not traumatic. I was not in dire
need of medical attention. I was not, even, in need of saving. I
push against the labels because they take away my own power
and agency. I knew what position to be in. I had taken care of my
body and my body was capable. The fact that I wasn't surrounded
by medical personnel did not make birth dangerous. The situation, in fact, never felt unsafe to me. I wasn't afraid. Rather, I was
aware of my body and of what I needed to do.

Would my telling of the story be different if things hadn't
turned out as well—if our son didn't breathe, or if the cord had
wrapped around his neck or got stuck? Of course. A friend gently
tells me that childbirth *is* traumatic, and based on one defini-
tion—a life-changing event that requires physical and emotional
recovery—my friend is right. But why the word "trauma"? Why
do we overlook the fact that, as Block reveals in *Pushed*, home
births have been proven to be just as safe for low-risk pregnancies

as hospital births (with 95 percent of five thousand women in one home birth study giving birth vaginally) and instead assume it's life threatening? Though certainly intense, certainly transformative, and certainly profound in a way that belies our ability to capture it in words, birth does not strip women of agency. It does not make them victims, flat on their backs in a hospital bed, incapable of making healthy decisions on their own and unworthy of respect and support.

Each week it seems another article comes out. According to the World Health Organization, UNICEF, and a slew of other organizations, the United States has the highest maternal mortality rate among developed countries. The United States is one of the few countries in the world to have experienced an increase in maternal mortality since 1990. The CDC reports that 43 percent of mothers suffer from "morbidity" during childbirth, defined as any departure from "a state of physiological or psychological well-being," and nursing professor Cheryl Beck, who studies the psychological fallout of childbirth, has reported that 1.5 to 6 percent of mothers experience post-traumatic stress disorder as a result of their birth experiences.

"You can tell a lot from the way women tell their birth stories," my doula says to me during my postpartum meeting. "I think we all need therapy," a midwife I later interview says. I listen to them. And I listen to my friends, whose birth stories are proud and yet often tinted with regret: the long-lasting side effects of their emergency C-sections, the failure of their bodies, their losses of control.

In a culture that views birth as inherently traumatic rather than women as inherently powerful, my friends are mourning something they shouldn't have to mourn.

CONCLUSION

My body wasn't medicalized. It wasn't a series of numbers. It was quaking, tense, opening. It was a jaw on the mattress of a bed. It was power and thrust and force and blood. It was uninhibited and beautifully untethered.

A COST ACCOUNTING
OF ЗIRTH

BIPEDALISM

In contrast to the Old Testament, which blamed the pain of childbirth on sin, evolutionary biologists in the late twentieth century proposed the Obstetrical Dilemma: the human birth process was difficult and dangerous because the baby's encephalitic head had to pass through a mother's bipedal birth canal. They said the change in pelvic shape when humans began to walk, and the increase in brain size of the infant, pushed the birthing process to the edge of what was possible.

It's an edge most birthing women have experienced. "The ring of fire," they say of the moment the infant's head crowns. Each of the times I give birth—clenching and shuddering on a hospital bed, and later biting the edge of a mattress—my body burns and rips and I think, *This is what it feels like to die. I'm going to die. My body can't do this.*

CRANIUM

The newborn cranium, broken into five not-yet-ossified plates that shift and slide against each other, protects a brain that is only 28 percent of its adult size, unlike most other mammals, who by birth have already developed at least 40 percent of their adult brains. Baby gorillas are blessed with 45 percent of their adult brains. The domestic llama, 72 percent.

Despite its relative smallness, however, the human infant's cranium barely escapes the bones of the birth canal—a tighter fit, biologists admit, than most other primates.

DANGERS

When I am pregnant, health practitioners give me a long list of things to avoid, including but not limited to caffeine, alcohol, unpasteurized cheese, sushi, excessive exercise, and almost any medication stronger than Tylenol. I pee in a cup before each appointment, and midway through each pregnancy, I am told to drink a thick sugary drink that makes me nauseous and brings on a migraine, all to test if I have gestational diabetes. I don't, but as my blood pressure ticks up, the nurses frown and say we'll have to watch for preeclampsia.

I'm not afraid of childbirth, but there is fear in this room, and it seems the danger is me.

DEATH

In *Brought to Bed: Childbearing in America, 1750–1950*, Judith Walzer Leavitt describes childbearing as a "shadow" that followed women throughout their childbearing years: "Young women perceived that their bodies, even when healthy and vigorous, could yield up a dead infant or could carry the seeds of their own destruction."

They of course had a reason. Early in the twentieth century, one mother died for every 154 births. Which means that from a group of thirty young women, childbirth would kill at least one.

FISTULAS

In addition to death, women often feared physical debility. Some women suffered from vesicovaginal or rectovaginal fistulas, holes between the vagina and either the bladder or the rectum. Before physicians knew to repair these holes—and before Dr. J. Marion Sims, the "Father of Modern Gynecology," perfected the procedure by practicing on enslaved African Americans—women simply suffered, living the rest of their lives with urine or feces leaking through the vaginal opening, impossible to control.

Leavitt writes that some of these fistulas resulted from "the violence of childbirth." Others, however, were caused by forceps, the metal tool physicians clamped around the emerging infant's head. Sometimes the forceps punctured the infant's skull. Sometimes they tore through the woman's flesh.

GESTATION

It makes no sense. For nine months, the fetus spins and kicks and shifts and grows in the womb. One would think, as its head grows to the point where it may not escape, that the female body would simply evict it earlier. Too big for the door? Out you go!

Evolutionary biologists, however, have disproved the Obstetrical Dilemma: a pelvis large enough to accommodate a newborn's head would not, actually, limit a woman's ability to walk. Instead, they suggest that metabolism, perhaps even more than the pelvis, constrains fetal brain growth and triggers labor. By the end of a full-term pregnancy, the mother simply cannot consume enough calories to support both herself and the fetus.

HEALTH

When I am fourteen weeks pregnant with my second child and less than excited about the oncoming birth, my OB suggests that an ultrasound might cheer me. She squeezes gel onto my belly, lowers the wand, and smiles as the fetus flickers before us. "See!" she says. "Doesn't that help?"

I am supposed to say yes. I am supposed to say the pain and discomfort of pregnancy are worth it and that the costs of bearing children pay off. That pregnancy creates a glow and is joyous. That infants are adorably cute and add meaning to life. And maybe that's enough, and maybe they do. But as I leave the clinic—heavier than when I came in and holding a photograph that reveals how my body is being used—I begin to suspect the cost-benefit analysis is more complicated than that.

INVESTMENT

In "Human Evolution and the Helpless Infant," Wenda Trevathan and Karen Rosenberg describe how newborns, though more helpless than monkeys and apes, employ "unusual behavior" that endears them to others. Fresh out of the womb, newborns scrunch their arms into their bodies, stare, and smile. Their chubby faces have an almost universal appeal. Meanwhile, oxytocin and socio-endocrinological transformations alter the mother's "affiliative responses." Post-birth becomes "an opportune time for her infant to engage in ways that 'prove' that he is worth the prolonged investment that human young require."

JOURNEYING

That prolonged investment includes the need to carry young. African elephants, which emerge from their mother's birth canal with 38 percent of their brains developed, can quickly get on their feet and join their herd. Chimpanzee infants, born with 40 percent of their adult brains, can cling to a mother's body while she forages for food. Humans, on the other hand, with their meager

28 percent, can only grip a finger, nurse, and stare eight inches in front of their faces. In addition, their mothers' hairless vertical torsos further limit the newborn's capacity to hang on. The result: human babies are caught in a helpless state of "secondary altriciality" and require just as much metabolically in their "fourth trimester" as they do in the third.

KILOCALORIES

The Cost of Pregnancy: 300 kcal/day in the third trimester, for a total of 75,000 kcal.

The Cost of Breastfeeding: 500 kcal/day, for a total (on average) of 220,000 kcal throughout lactation.

LACTATION

Though primarily inert, as if hibernating, mammary glands awaken with reproduction. During pregnancy, blood flow to the breasts doubles. Estrogen and prolactin rise. Progesterone rises at the same time before decreasing at the end, a combination that makes maternal brains more receptive to "infantile cues." After birth, infant suckling triggers nerve pulses to the hypothalamus. Paraventricular neurons then project to the posterior pituitary. Oxytocin is released. Prolactin is released. Both travel to the mammary glands and bind to myoepithelial cells and lactocytes. This binding triggers the cells to contract, forcing milk through the ducts. Blood flow decreases and then suddenly increases a minute or so later, often causing the sensation of a tweak or a twinge.

The result, according to biologist Sarah B. Hrdy in *Costly and Cute: Helpless Infants and Human Evolution*: "With the onset of lactation, mothers are on a 'mammary leash,' endocrinologically incentivized to nurture and far less inclined to abandon an infant."

MAMMARY LEASH

When I am lactating, my glucose levels dip if I haven't eaten recently. My hands begin to shake and my thoughts scatter. Anyone talking to me is talking too loudly. I glare with daggers and push people away with my elbows. I reach for the refrigerator—for lactation cookies and yogurt and leftovers and sliced melon. I inhale them all, becoming a bearlike version of myself. I rumble through the house, leaving wrappers and empty Tupperware and peanut butter–coated spoons on the counter. Afterward, sated, with my son's lips clamped and pulsing on my breast, it strikes me with the certainty of a newly sharpened knife: my body will do what it needs to sustain itself and this child.

NERVES

At the turn of the twentieth century, concerned that affluent, educated (and largely white) women were increasingly experiencing physical debility and nervous breakdowns while pregnant, Dr. Franklin Newell of Harvard Medical School wrote: "It seems to me that this overdevelopment of the nervous organization [through education and modern life] is responsible for the increased morbidity of pregnancy and labor which is apparent among these women of the overcivilized class."

Dr. I. N. Love of St. Louis in 1883: "We all know that the pregnant woman is prone to having her nervous system out of joint; in fact, the condition in itself is a severe test to the female nervous system. It is needless to recall to your mind how the very beginning of pregnancy is announced in many cases by peculiar nervous phenomena. During the entire term the imagination of the woman often becomes exalted or depressed. Her disposition is irritable. In many cases she is continually between two fires; upon the one side the greatest gloom, upon the other an excessive joy. Suspicion, jealousy, general sensitiveness are present, which under other conditions are never dreamed of. Nervous pains abound, migraine, facial neuralgia, toothache, itching in various parts of the body, together with smarting and other evidence of irritation of the peripheral extremities of the nerves."

OBSTETRICS

Newell and Love were two of the nation's first obstetricians, the field that emerged in the 1880s when physicians began taking over home births, long overseen by midwives, and birthing women eventually moved into hospitals. Most obstetricians, like Newell and Love, believed menstruation made women the weaker sex.

Many women believed physicians like Newell and Love were more learned and had access to a knowledge that women and midwives did not. Physicians offered forceps, which saved women from complicated deliveries. They also offered pain medication: laudanum, ether, and chloroform.

Women, fearful of the pain of birth, were often interested in pain medication—in the way they could simply go to the hospital, fall asleep, and wake up with an infant, everything over.

PUERPERAL INFECTION

That is, unless they didn't wake up. In the 1800s and 1900s, birthing women were plagued by puerperal fever, a bacterial infection in the uterus. It is estimated that most cases of puerperal fever were transmitted by physicians and early obstetricians who did not yet understand germ theory and carried the bacteria on hands they plunged into women's cervixes or on the metal planes of their forceps. The mass migration to hospitals, in fact, caused an increase in maternal death. Maternal deaths did not actually decline until the discovery of antibiotics.

PUERPERAL INFECTION, REVISITED

In 2017, NPR and ProPublica shocked the world with a report on maternal mortality. Although the United Kingdom, Canada, and France all boasted maternal death rates below 10 for every 100,000 live births, the United States's rate had doubled over the past twenty-five years and now rested at 26.4, with rates particularly high for Black women and women of color.

According to NPR, "Babies are monitored more closely than mothers during and after birth," and although a baby is "whisked off" to a neonatal unit at the first sign of trouble, hospital staff overlook maternal complications, expecting the mother to be fine.

QUESTIONS

I do not want to fall into the trap of biological determinism or essentialism and imply that mothers have no agency or choice: that human biology simply results in a difficult birth; that mothers are strung out and dictated by hormones they cannot control. I do not want to imply that Dr. Love is at all justified in his observation that pregnant women are "nervous." He is not.

But still, I have questions. Questions that sometimes keep me up in the dark, quiet periods between my infant's night wakings.

If pregnancy and birth can, indeed, be painful and dangerous, is there some truth to the story the Old Testament tells about Eve? Are women inherently resigned to a difficult lot?

If pregnancy and birth can, indeed, be painful and dangerous, and if caretaking exhausts us, does this mean that women are weak and in need of assistance?

If I don't want to see myself as weak or in need of assistance, am I ignoring the very real ways my childbearing body demands others' support?

What does it mean to have a body that asks so much of me?

What does it mean if it means nothing at all?

RESPECT

On YouTube, one can find birthing videos. Videos of vaginal births and C-sections, videos of home births or hospital births with women dazed from epidurals. Videos of women squatting and videos of women screaming. The videos of women screaming seem to get the most hits, with viewers commenting, "Anyone else get turned on?"

Other videos are softer. In one, a woman gives birth by a river or creek. In the video, she squats and kneels and prostrates herself on a yoga mat that rests on river rock. Birds chirp in the background. She is quiet save a few soft grunts and some panting near the end. No one, until the delivery, aids her. In a statement that stays with me because I long for that experience myself, she writes, "It was the singular most transforming event of my life and my most conscious act as a woman to date."

SUPPORT

Prior to the overtaking of birth by male physicians, Leavitt says, most women gave birth at home, tended by trained midwives and female relatives and friends who would often stay for days or weeks, helping with household tasks and caretaking. The women celebrated life together. They suffered and mourned their losses together. They created a "social childbirth" that "united women and provided…one of the functional bonds that formed the basis of women's domestic culture."

In *Costly and Cute*, Wenda Trevathan and Karen Rosenberg argue that the only way the human species could have survived and sustained itself, considering the demands of reproduction and child-rearing, was by developing just this type of social bond: a system of extensive, cooperative caretaking that involved an entire community, not just parents.

TAMARINS

Tamarins, from the family Callitrichidae, are also a social species of primates, requiring cooperative breeding and biparental care. It isn't unusual for tamarin groups to consist of a half dozen or so males and more than one female, and all of the tamarins help raise the young.

In fact, if a pregnant or birthing tamarin does not sense she has enough assistance, she has been known to drop her infant on the ground and, if that fails to elicit a community response, to on rare occasions even bite the baby's face and devour its brains.

In "Of Marmosets, Men, and the Transformative Power of Babies," Sarah B. Hrdy says humans aren't so different; "Callitrichine and human mothers have converged on a similar decision rule: proactively line up allomaternal assistance, but if that fails, bail out."

When my husband and I discussed having a child, our discussions were not often about some innate desire for children but rather resources. Did we have sufficient health insurance? Could we afford day care? Did we have family or friends nearby who could babysit? Did we have the energy to get through those sleepless nights? Each time we deliberated, I hesitated at our already tight budget, our distance from relatives, our demanding careers, and paused at the uncertainties, ready to abandon the venture.

Later, with my son crying, and my daughter crying, and my husband half an hour away at work, and no one else in our two-thousand-square-foot house but me, ragged from a lack of sleep, hands on my cell phone without anyone to call, I pause again, like a tamarin in a tree, and recognize the impulse to dash and bail out.

UNCERTAINTIES

Today, one human mother dies for every 3,788 births. Most of those deaths are from hemorrhage and preeclampsia. Some 60 percent of those deaths could be prevented. Which of course means 40 percent could not. The American Pregnancy Association includes a webpage on how to write a will. A 2017 Department of Agriculture report estimates the cost of raising a child to age seventeen to be $233,610. Genesis still warns: "I will greatly multiply thy sorrow and thy conception; in sorrow thou shalt bring forth children."

VALUE

When I look at my body—a body that has felt a fetus's soft kicks and the shift of an almost fully formed butt against the stretched skin of my belly, a body that has watched those large lumps move from side to side, a body that has felt an infant's mouth latch onto my nipple before letting go in milky exhaustion, a body that has experienced the painful twinge of a letdown of milk and woken to a wet shirt, a body scarred with stretch marks and an inverted belly button—when I look at that body and ask, *What does it mean to be a childbearing woman?*, what I really want to know is what happens when the ideologies and structures we've used to understand our lives all fall away. Gender. Biology. Medicine. Religion. Does this take away some of the value we've given birth and women, or does it allow us to see things clearly? What words do we use to describe childbirth then? What tales do we tell?

WORTH

Men have told me the pains of childbirth are a punishment, and that women are weak and animallike and can be discredited as hormonal, and that pregnancy is a pathologic process that requires careful monitoring in a hospital where we can pretend, for a brief moment, that the body can be controlled.

But what if birth simply is as it is—an infant's head nearing the point where it can't fit, metabolic costs tipping into instability—and my ability to give birth is solely that: an ability to give birth. Not a power struggle but the purely physical. The pelvis. The birth canal. The hard surface of bone. The red and veined placenta. The process that sometimes benefits from human assistance—that has evolved, in fact, from human assistance—but also will continue expelling infants all on its own.

WORDS

Though maybe that's what terrifies us the most. How, when viewed over eons, childbirth erases us. Plunges us into a timeline where silence is better than words. Man? Woman? You? Me? It doesn't matter. Just the ordinary, extraordinary need of the body to survive.

TO HATCH INTIMACY
FROM DESPAIR

The early months of my son's life are like whiplash, a sometimes daily wrenching between health and despair. Often I am happy, content, fully a part of myself. I dance with my son in the living room, I smile at him while he nurses, I tickle his fat thighs while changing his diaper, I go on walks in the mild afternoons, enjoying the wind on my face, his heart-shaped mouth puckered. He squawks when the wind blows or the sun suddenly escapes from a cloud, but he is otherwise quiet. We've done it, I think. We've managed to get through the worst unscathed. Prenatal depression is a memory, further and further away, and I know I have escaped it.

But sometimes a darkness overtakes me, quiet and quick. One minute I am fine—I recognize myself—and the next I want to crawl into the closet and hide behind the clothes. I know that in having him I have made a terrible mistake. My son cries in his bassinet. My four-year-old daughter calls to me from the other room, but rather than go to them I cry in the bathroom. In bed. Deep, sudden, shuddering sobs, and I can feel myself slipping, my forearms shredding from rough rock as I try to grab ahold of something. I lay in bed longer than I should. I wonder, in a paralyzing way, how far I have to go to lose myself completely. I look out at the driveway, the trees, the blueish green horizon, and I know I could do it: pack a suitcase, start walking, and never return.

How do you love a child you did not want?

My son's pregnancy is unplanned—a loss of control—a fertilization after I said I was done. It is confusion, and numbness, my mind hovering three feet above my skin, until I don't know who I am anymore. This woman in the doctor's office, being told "congratulations"? Or the woman who for six months can't say "I'm pregnant" without crying (and thus doesn't say anything at all)?

I remove myself from my life. Too exhausted and nauseous to do anything else, I spend most of my time laying on the couch, falling into a deeper despair.

My husband calls me a walking zombie. I bring my daughter to day care later and later each day. I don't always shower. When I do shower, I take long showers, letting the water run down and down my back, sometimes so hot it nearly scalds me. I try to make myself feel something. Anything. I stare at my stomach, starting to bloat and push out. I stare at myself. I spend far too much time staring at myself, not quite recognizing the exhausted face I see in front of me. I keep waking at 3 a.m., terrified that my lack of excitement means I am going to be a terrible mother.

When I was pregnant with my daughter, I spent my Friday and Saturday mornings navigating neighborhood garage sales in search of twenty-five-cent onesies. I'd collect them, and then lay them on the dining room table at home to show off to my husband: a promising pile of pastels.

When I am pregnant with my son, I can hardly stand infant clothing. I avoid garage sales and the baby section of Target. Joy is so far from the picture, I hide in the bedroom when my husband announces the pregnancy to his family. "I'm tired," I say. "I need to take a nap." But really, I can't stand their remarks or pretend that I am happy.

When the diagnosis of prenatal depression eventually comes, it is only an additional loss of control. I am a sad, broken specimen of a mother, pitied and flawed. My body has been wrenched from me as well as my mind.

To quell my self-blame, I read what I can. Midwife Ina May Gaskin tells me, "Most—but not all—cases of postpartum depression and postpartum psychosis can be prevented by providing plenty of help to new mothers during the weeks following birth....Mothering is sometimes the loneliest job around, but it shouldn't be."

Depression expert Andrew Solomon tells me, "We have not acknowledged how appropriately anxiety-ridden pregnancy is, how traumatic the change in identity that accompanies prospective motherhood can be." And thus women—depressed or otherwise—feel judged when they aren't "high on hormones."

Even the medical journals assert that most prenatal and postpartum depression risk factors are situational rather than hormonal. An unplanned pregnancy. A lack of social support. Relationship issues. Life changes. Isolation.

All of which I can identify in myself. My son's pregnancy was unplanned. My family had just moved to a new state. My husband and I had disagreed about whether to have another child. In our new city, we hadn't yet established a community of close friends.

Yet the dilemma remains: *How do you love a child you did not want?*

My son's soft kicks hint at an attachment I register but can't embrace.

In the months after my son is born, I occasionally spend time on an online forum dedicated to women with prenatal or postpartum depression. The stories are heartbreaking. Women in utter despair at the way they feel about motherhood. Women plagued by intrusive thoughts that make them afraid to be alone with their children. Women who don't know what is happening to them or who to talk to. Women who want to go back to work, or are afraid of going back to work, or want other kids, or are afraid of having other kids because their postpartum experience with their first was so haunting.

Some women debate whether to check themselves in to mental facilities. They debate whether to leave their spouses. They debate whether they can continue one more day. They say they have no one to talk to. They are stuck with crying children, and they can't take it.

On my worst days—when the house becomes a cage, eerily electric, and my son is a leech who demands more and more of my body—I find the conversations comforting. I am not alone. On my better days, I hold the stories at a distance, afraid to be sucked back into despair. But I am also humbled. So many stories out in the world. So many difficult and often silenced stories.

That winter, I come across Lily Gurton-Wachter's "The Stranger Guest," an overview of the literature of motherhood, published in the *LA Book Review*. In the article, Gurton-Wachter compares the literature of war—seen as worthy of both male and female audiences—with the literature of motherhood, which is often ignored or relegated to only women, even though the experience of motherhood is just as transformative, and often just as haunting, as the experience of a soldier.

Most interesting to me, Gurton-Wachter identifies how difficult it is to capture the reality of early motherhood: "This is a paradox already familiar to critics and scholars of war literature: extreme experiences tend to evade explanation or even description, and the writer able to understand and give a full account of what happened is often not the one who has suffered it most forcefully. In the context of parenting, this manifests as a problem of timing. By the time a new mother has the time (or free hands) to write again, the most extreme experience is beginning to fade from her memory."

That winter and spring, I keep hearing about the diagnoses of my friends. Three of them, all with young children, tell me they have postpartum depression. Another friend describes her and her partner's childcare arrangements. She works during the day, her partner at night, and so they just hand off the child, and she is tired, and feels stuck, and recognizes that she and her wife haven't had a moment together since their daughter was born, and she mourns her writing life, yet she can't put her daughter in childcare. How could they afford it? I listen and feel beneath her words a familiar desperation, and I want to tell her to get some childcare and to protect that dimension of herself—and I try to—yet I know we are all caught in these internal struggles.

The first two years after my daughter was born, my identity often felt just out of reach. I was still a student in graduate school, but my daughter spent most of her time with me save a couple of hours with a babysitter each week. I remember being quickly frustrated. Sometimes bored. I spent a lot of time on my phone while nursing her. I spent a lot of time thinking about how to fill the days. Pushing her on the swing in the park. Talking in my head to no one. If I was depressed, it wasn't the hopeless despair I experienced with my son, but something milder. And maybe that just happens to all parents. The sudden shift and struggle to figure out who you are, now that your identity, indeed, has become something dripping and new.

Yet I also note how little room women are given for discontent. How little room we have to question society's conception of motherhood itself.

I protect my career after the birth of my son. I enroll him in day care, even during the summer, and give myself time to write. I soften, fully myself, in those hours, my fingers quick and sure on keyboard, my shoulders relaxed and still.

Nonetheless, I have to keep explaining myself. "No, I'm not teaching summer courses. No, I don't have to be on campus. Yes, I'm still taking the kids to day care." I begin to brace myself against the resulting raised eyebrows, and when I pull up to my son's day care in the afternoons—jittery, tense, jaw half-clenched—I force my face to smile.

I begin to think:
I do not want to be with him all day.
(I may not want to be with him at all.)
I have failed him as a mother.

On the postpartum discussion forums, women discuss ITs—the "intrusive thoughts" that have long characterized postpartum mood disorders and sometimes mark an edging into postpartum psychosis.

The women are scared, and only rarely do they actually type out their thoughts, but the thoughts range from the minor and hypothetical—"What if my baby choked?"—to "I wish my baby choked" or "It would be better if my baby died."

The thoughts terrify the women. They blame themselves for having them. And yet the thoughts continue.

One day, the moderator suggests we all read social worker Karen Kleiman and psychologist Amy Wenzel's *Dropping the Baby and Other Scary Thoughts*, which defines intrusive thoughts as "any worry, rumination, thought, obsession, misinterpretations, image, or impulse that feels inconsistent with whom a woman believes herself to be and causes a significant degree of anxiety or distress." In the book, Kleiman and Wenzel provide a long list of typical ITs / "scary thoughts," including, What if I drop the baby down the stairs? What if he stops breathing in the night? What if I press so hard on his soft spot that it crushes his skull? What if I feel like this forever and never get better? What if I'm a bad parent and ruin my child? What if I get so mad I shake the baby? If others knew what was in my head, they would think I am evil. I could just snap her little neck with such little effort. I could pull off his limbs and see the blood spurting all over the place. No one could possibly understand what I am feeling. I'm not sure I even love my baby. I don't want to be a mother.

"This is not an easy list to read," Kleiman and Wenzel write in conclusion.

Kleiman and Wenzel's book claws at me, largely because it is so accurate. Although my own intrusive thoughts are limited to regret over having my child and concerns that I've ruined my and my family's lives, I can relate to the rapid mood swings— euphoria to hopelessness—the shame, guilt, and "crushing sense of failure" that accompanies postpartum mood disorders, and the ways many women resist treatment because a diagnosis would only seem to confirm their status as terrible mothers. Reading the book, the realities of my own postpartum mental state stare back at me. I cannot deny it, and the weight of the experience—my own experience—presses like a barbell on my throat.

Yet parts of the book ignite a flinty anger. Despite their attempt to normalize intrusive thoughts, Kleiman and Wenzel describe postpartum women as "hormonally compromised": "When women are weakened by childbirth, the demands of the post-partum period, or anxious or depressive symptoms, they are easily wounded and defenseless against the attacks of the inner critic."

I do not appreciate being described as weak or compromised. I do not appreciate being described as ill or abnormal. And although I recognize that rumination sometimes prevents me from engaging stressful situations in proactive ways, I do not think the situation itself—the baby crying, my body straining to be anywhere but here—is merely a problem of perception.

Kleiman and Wenzel's tendency to disregard thoughts of dissatisfaction—"I do not want to be a mother"—and write them off as products of depression is unhelpful because, in my case at least, the thoughts *are* true. Depressed or not, I had an unintended pregnancy. I hadn't actually wanted another child.

The most common treatments for ITs include therapy and medication. Midway through my pregnancy—*I do not want this baby. I'm going to be a terrible mother. I am going to ruin both of our lives*—my therapist sent me to my OB, where I cried, admitting my depression. I cried because I was ashamed, because I didn't think I could survive five more months of constant despair and hopelessness, but I also wanted the baby to be okay. My doctor prescribed an antidepressant and said she'd fax the prescription to my pharmacy. Five minutes after my confession, she exited and closed the door.

One of the most heartbreaking things Andrew Solomon describes in "The Secret Sadness of Pregnancy with Depression" is the struggle over medication. In a culture where pregnancy brings on "a universal Lent in which a thousand talismanic things must be forsaken for the health of the developing child," most women avoid antidepressants. Many doctors also avoid them, citing studies that have linked SSRIs with a heightened risk of miscarriage, preterm birth, and neonatal lung conditions. Some studies even suggest that antidepressants can lead to developmental abnormalities once the infant is an adolescent.

And yet, untreated prenatal depression itself has risks. Other studies have linked prenatal depression with miscarriage, preterm birth, and neonatal complications. The cortisol the fetus develops in can lead to cognitive impairments, delayed language development, and an increased risk of anxiety.

The lists of risks bear eerie resemblances. If some antidepressants have been linked with poor birth outcomes, and yet proceeding with a pregnancy while depressed has also been linked with poor birth outcomes, what is a mother to do? The sense that you are screwed if you take the medications and screwed if you don't haunts women, whose greatest fear, Solomon reports, tends to be that their depression will hurt their infants.

The majority of the postpartum depression threads I visit grapple with this very issue. Women ask, desperately, for stories from others who took antidepressants while pregnant and nonetheless gave birth to healthy infants. Others ask for advice on how to "white-knuckle it" and proceed using holistic means. The women don't want to be depressed, and they don't want to take medication, and they don't want to potentially harm their infants, but they also want to be okay.

For three days, I weighed my options, feeling like a failure either way. On the third day, just before a trip out of town, anxious that my mood might plummet to a depth I couldn't get out of alone, I stopped at the pharmacy, only to discover that my OB had either forgotten to fax the prescription or had faxed it somewhere else. Back in the parking lot, empty-handed, my hands shook on the steering wheel. I didn't know whether to sob or sigh with relief.

Although I eventually drove away, I continued to fear I wouldn't love my child enough. And that—the fear that I wouldn't love him enough—lingered even after his birth.

Andrew Solomon: "Most who battle antenatal or postpartum depression are committed to their children, and are trying to commit to the identity that is motherhood. For some expectant mothers and new parents, love seems to be automatic; it wafts them instantly up to a new level of consciousness. Others have to climb a very steep staircase to reach the same heights. The fact that the exercise can be agonizing and that some women cannot quite make it does not dull the intent behind it. Depression calls on resources some women have and some women don't, including a capacity to hatch intimacy out of despair. Wanting to love your child is not the same thing as loving your child, but there is a lot of love even in the wanting."

On his first birthday, the experience of loving my son is an ache. I watch him eat banana slices off of the floor and I want to cry, because he is beautiful and it hurts to watch, and it hurts to watch because I know what the year has asked of me.

I know that I didn't want another child. I know that I have nonetheless taken care of one. I know that, in the long evenings of my son's infancy, I have gone to him, pulling open my pajamas. I have rocked and nursed him in the cold, quiet of the house, his mouth pulling milk, his eyes glazed. I have held him softly. The biology has taken over. I am helpless before it.

Does accepting and coming to love him, despite my experience of prenatal depression and the fact that I never enjoyed his infancy, erase the version of myself who struggled so much and legitimately questioned whether she should have another child in the first place? Does coming to love him prove everyone else right: that my despair over the overwhelming tasks of motherhood was just depression—"all in my head"—and that mothers must sacrifice for their children? That it, indeed, is honorable to sacrifice for your children?

In the past year, people have told me that eventually none of this will matter. Postpartum depression will recede and I will realize I loved him all along and that we have a strong bond. Or postpartum depression was to blame, but it will lift and it is not who I am, as if postpartum depression is some fog-like substance that comes and leaves and any guilt or dissatisfaction with motherhood will recede with it.

For the most part, I believe them. I know I will get to know my son, his personality becoming more and more vivid and precious, until one day I won't be able to imagine life without him. The memories will accumulate enough to where I am only grateful for his existence, in the way I am already grateful for the experience of his infancy and how it has made me more humble, compassionate, and empathetic toward the invisible anguish of others.

Yet such comments also remind me of the pro-life, anti-abortion stories I sometimes come across in which a woman who became a mother as a result of rape describes how grateful she is for her child.

The stories are an emotional appeal, of course. Even in cases of rape, they tell us, children are a blessing, and mothers will and should love them. And I do believe that those mothers have come to love their children. I believe the way the mothers wrap an arm around their children's shoulders. I believe their loving gaze.

But those anecdotes are not actually about abortion. They are about resilience. Yes, that woman has come to love and accept her child. But would you really want her not to? Would you really want her to spend eighteen-plus years detached and resentful? We find meaning and make narratives from our lives. But our ability to accept and respond to our realities does not mean those realities are ideal, acceptable, or inherently okay. Our ability to be resilient does not make the trauma "right." It does not erase the experience itself.

Sometimes I think about the past two years—from the moment I peed on a stick and discovered I was pregnant to my son's first birthday—and try to rewrite the story. I analyze those months before and after his conception and try to convince myself that I *did* want him all along—that deep down, my own, pure desire for another child is what compelled me, unconsciously, to make the decisions I did. I search and I search, as if finding that storyline could give me a cleaner and easier narrative to share.

But my hands are empty. There is no easy narrative to share. Only the truth. I didn't want to be pregnant. I dreaded his pregnancy and birth. But I nonetheless proceeded. I was ambivalent and full of fear, but I made that choice.

I return to Andrew Solomon's article. To his statement that depression calls on women to hatch intimacy from despair, and that some women can't.

I return to Ina May Gaskin and all of those who hint that postpartum depression may be a reaction to alienation and isolation more than a disorder itself—that there's a difference between a pathological psyche and a pathological situation.

I return to Kleiman and Wenzel. *I don't want this baby. He's better off dead. No one could possibly understand how I'm feeling.*

I return to my son, crawling on the floor, lifting a chubby hand to ask earnestly for milk.

How do you love a child you didn't want? I've stopped asking the question because an answer doesn't exist. Yet this, too, is true:

Slowly and surely, a speckled shell can crack. Mottled and throbbing and fierce.

BIRTH WORK
IN THE BIBLE BELT

"I named my company Birth by Design to reflect the way God designed women to give birth," Nicolle tells me. We are sitting in one of Conway's Christian coffee shops, and even though I've heard Nicolle's story before, I can't help but flinch.

When I first met Nicolle, the founder of Conway's largest doula agency, I was eleven weeks pregnant with my second child, struggling to navigate my own birth options in Arkansas and to figure out what it meant to bring forth a child in a community where social groups formed primarily through churches. Though I, myself, had been raised in a religious family, most churches in Minnesota were Catholic or Lutheran rather than Baptist, and regardless, you didn't talk about religion with others. Furthermore, I'd largely broken from Catholicism by the time I arrived in Arkansas—slowly repelled by its teachings on female sexuality and women's secondary place in the church.

As a result, I found Nicolle's evangelical approach to birth disorienting. The United States's maternal death rate had recently catapulted to one of the highest in the developed world, and Arkansas ranked among the five worst states. The reasons for the spike: an overreliance on interventions and lack of support for the needs and wishes of birthing women. Indeed, more and more women were reporting birth trauma, caused when medical professionals forced them to have interventions, some of which could prolong their recovery and leave them with physical and emotional scars.

In this context, surely the most effective advocacy in the South would look less like Birth by Design, with its pastel-colored crucifix centered on the office wall and its adherence to male-dominated Christianity, and more like the Farm Midwifery Center, a birthing center in Tennessee that began when a caravan of eighty buses and more than three hundred "hippie idealists" settled on a rural cattle farm in 1970. Women at the Farm gave birth in earth shelters and birth cabins, and images on the Farm's website continue to depict long-haired women birthing and breastfeeding uninhibited. There is no mention of Christianity.

Yet, as I sit with Nicolle and listen to her story—first as her client, and now as a writer with unanswered questions about feminism, Christianity, and birth work in the South—I'm struck again and again by how closely her woman-centered motivation mirrors that of the Farm's renowned midwife, Ina May Gaskin.

One of the few Black birth workers in Arkansas, Nicolle has made a name for herself in Conway. She trains countless doulas, leads a prenatal dance class, and attends nearly two dozen births a year. She seems to know every mother in the city of sixty thousand, and in fact greets at least three of them during our interview, her voice booming with warm recognition each time. When I first moved to Conway and met her, it was this confidence that stood out to me. Nicolle claims her space—not afraid to hide her body size, her exuberance, her faith, or her passions— and although it is clear from an occasional, haggard tension in her tone that the toll of working in largely white medical spaces, with largely white medical professionals, has worn on her, she remains deeply committed to her work.

As young adults hunch over Bibles at the tables around us, Nicolle tells me that before she started Birth by Design, women who sought a natural, unmedicated birth tended to "evacuate" Conway. They, along with women in the surrounding communities, would drive up to an hour and a half to Little Rock just to avoid the hospitals in their hometowns and have a little bit of control over their bodies and their births.

"And I say a 'little bit of control,' right?" Nicolle adds. "What I've seen is women not having control. Woman, after their water broke, weren't allowed to get out of bed, for fear of prolapsed cord. Well, that's interesting, because there's less than a 1 percent chance of that even happening. So their water ruptured, and they were forced to stay in bed under continuous monitoring. After they checked into the hospital, it was almost like they were prisoners, not even able to get up to use the bathroom. They'd have to use the bedpan. And when the pain became unbearable because they couldn't move, we'd just control it with the epidural. So there were high epidural rates and high C-section rates."

Many women, Nicolle says, were told their pelvises were too small and checked off as "failure to progress" simply because they weren't able to get up and move, which would have allowed the baby to shift into a better position. Some of the doctors would lie to their patients, telling them that they weren't dilating and needed a C-section even though the nurses had just checked them and said they were progressing just fine. But what frustrated Nicolle the most was a lack of change. Women complained, she says, but not to the right people. Women would even go back to the same doctors when pregnant again.

Since starting Birth by Design, Nicolle has labored to create

birth-positive communities in Central Arkansas, and she's worked
hard to cultivate relationships with doctors and nurses in order
to do so. She has doctors on speed dial now, and she has spoken
to them outside of the delivery room about birth philosophy.
More and more of Conway's doctors support doula-assisted, unmedicated births and vaginal births after C-sections (VBACs),
including doctors who snubbed all of those before.

"But there are definitely doctors who are now even more
locked into a corner and say unmedicated births are crazy, or 'go
buy a fancy stroller instead of having a doula,'" Nicolle says. "And
women are still coming to us and saying, 'Is it okay for me to hire
you? I just want to make sure it's okay with my doctor that I hire
you.'"

Nicolle blames these responses on our society's tendency to
view birth as under the jurisdiction of physicians rather than as
a meaningful experience of the mother's. A mother of three and
the wife of a local evangelical minister, Nicolle says her calling is
to place birth back in the hands of women.

My first birth, in upstate New York, took place in a private
Catholic hospital, where in addition to doctors, I had the op-
tion to work with one of two midwives: a Jewish woman who
had served at the hospital for decades or her protégé, a tall thin
redhead who wore a small cross around her neck. The city also
had a public hospital, but the Catholic hospital was closer to our
apartment and had a better reputation for supporting midwifery
and unmedicated births. Nonetheless, I remember feeling wary.
Did I want to give birth in a facility that would never offer abortions? Did I want to give birth in a facility that may even shun
birth control?

In Arkansas, the midwife-barring hospital I utilized when

pregnant with my son was not affiliated with a religious institution, but religious brochures sat in each of the waiting rooms, and
when I told my ob-gyn that I'd had a few glasses of wine before
discovering I was pregnant with my second child, she chuckled
and said, "That's just the Lord's way of letting you have one last
good time."

For some reason, this atmosphere bothered me more. Perhaps
because Evangelicalism was foreign to me, whereas Catholicism
was at least familiar. Perhaps more simply because Evangelicalism
was ever present. In Conway, the Southern Baptist churches ri-
valed the size of the local high school, my daughter's day care required all children to pray before snack time, and a yoga teacher
at the public library occasionally played Christian worship music
during free community classes. I was constantly aware of the societal role I was supposed to be playing—the heterosexual married mother—and because I was, indeed, heterosexual, married,
and a mother, I did not always know how to push against those
pressures. I was a nonbeliever in a city of believers. A questioning academic in a community of church-attending moms. As I
prepared to birth my son and researched birth trends across the
nation, I wanted to criticize the evangelical birth culture I saw
around me. But I couldn't. I recognized myself as an outsider—
an unknowing stranger—and I knew I had a lot to learn about
the realities of birth work in the South.

Not long after interviewing Nicolle, I pull into the driveway of
community midwife Kim Jacobs, one of the women Nicolle works
closely with in her plight to improve birth options in Arkansas.
Kim has left the door unlocked for me while she finishes a home
visit, so I let myself into a 1950s ranch-style house, decorated in a
manner best described as "pastel country chic." Blue, mauve, and

orange pillows decorate the couches, and the late morning light
fills the room with a quiet glow.

A few minutes later, a garage door rumbles and I am greeted
by a middle-aged Caucasian woman with a warm smile and a
striking asymmetrical haircut. Immediately, I regret not scheduling a consultation with her when I was pregnant. Kim reminds
me very much of my daughter's preschool teacher—motherly,
compassionate, and inviting—but with a progressive twist.
Unlike Nicolle, Kim does not consider herself religious. Unlike
Nicolle, she is also introverted. When she speaks, I have to lean
forward to hear. Yet she exudes a quiet self-assurance.

In Conway, the most nonconformist birth is a home birth.
Only 0.9 percent of women in Conway currently elect this approach (the rest choose an ob-gyn at the hospital, where 38.8 percent of women end up with C-sections—just above the national
average, and well above the WHO's recommendation of 10 percent), but those who do tend to gravitate toward Kim. Originally
from Colorado, Kim has lived in Conway for more than a decade
and has become a pillar in the midwife community. She helps
organize an annual meeting of the state's midwives, and she
is actively involved in negotiations between the midwives and
the state's health department, currently embroiled over whether
home birth clients can refuse to go to the health department for
state-mandated vaginal exams.

As Kim tells me from her office, a side room with one wall of
bookcases, a desk, and another couch, the greatest barrier to better birth choices in Arkansas is fear. Women, doctors, and policymakers fear poor outcomes. "But because of how the hospitals
and their protocols and systems are set up," Kim says, "*people* are
causing the problems that people are afraid of."

As an example, she mentions the umbilical cord. "Everyone is afraid of the cord being around the neck. That's the wildest thing, because really, it's so normal. It's stretchy," she says. "It's meant to do what it does." The midwife simply has to watch the infant's head and shoulders as they emerge. If the cord looks tight, or if there appears to be a knot, she can somersault the baby or perform small maneuvers that keep the baby close to the cord and there are no issues. The issues, in fact, tend to occur as a result of *fear* of a tight cord, rather than a tight cord itself.

In the hospital, Kim says, someone checks for a cord. As the baby's head emerges, someone sticks a finger alongside the head, into the vagina. That finger disturbs the body, often causing the mother or the baby to involuntarily constrict. The mother or baby flinches, in other words, creating a vagal response that can result in a brief loss of consciousness. If the physician does feel a cord, he or she will then disturb the process even more by pulling the cord over the baby's head. This often causes another vagal response.

"So now we have caused the baby to be stunned, and the baby is born a bit floppy—essentially it has fainted—but because of this, because the baby is not crying or perfectly pink, they cut the cord fully and whisk the baby away. So the baby is on the other side of the room, to have stimulation. The parents are terrified, the baby is terrified, and it was all unnecessary. It was caused by the physician. But all physicians in the United States do it, so now every woman is terrified about the cord being around the neck."

In her initial meetings with Conway's clients, Kim spends a significant amount of time assuring women about these anxieties. Only 10 percent of her clients will need to be transferred to the hospital (usually because a long early labor has exhausted them), and only 4 percent of her clients have a cesarean. Nonetheless, every single one is scared of the what-ifs. "The idea is out there that birth is dangerous. That you are a time bomb ticking. That you have to be in the hospital because you might explode, and die, and your baby is going to die. Just because you are in labor."

I frown, recognizing this list of misconceptions from my own experience as well as from the articles I've read. Still, when I ask Kim how we can fix the problem and prevent women from even acquiring those fears, she only sighs.

Maybe better media representations of birth, she suggests. Maybe better birth education in schools, starting with our youth. But ultimately, it would require systemic change. We'd need to alter the way we view pregnant women, and we'd need to give them agency. "A weird thing happens when we're pregnant," Kim says, utterly perplexed. "People treat us like children, like all of a sudden, because we have a baby in our bodies, our brains malfunction and we can't think for ourselves and need to be told what to do. We have to be a *good girl*. There's definitely a paternalistic view, as if you don't know what's best for you."

She shakes her head and looks at me directly. "But nobody cares more about these women and their babies than they do themselves. No one is going to be more devastated at a bad outcome than the mother. So they should be able to choose which test procedures they want to do. They should be able to choose to have an assisted home birth. It's not anyone else's choice to make."

Talking about "choice" in Arkansas, of course, is a complicated matter. In 2016, 60.6 percent of Arkansans voted for Donald Trump. Although the reasons they did so resist quick summarization, many evangelicals ultimately voted as a result of abortion. Their first—and sometimes only—priority was a pro-life candidate. Within this culture, where abortion subsumes discussions of women's rights, birth advocates such as Kim and Nicolle find it difficult to raise awareness for birth options.

"Women will get up in arms about reproductive rights, which from what I'm understanding is the ability to have an abortion," Nicolle says. "So they can get up in arms about that, but when we talk about the actual birth, it's like, *forget the matter.* I don't know if it's because the loudest voices are not women that are birthing, but it frustrates me."

When I ask Nicolle why she doesn't think birthing women are speaking out more—insisting on their right to choose where they give birth, who attends them, and what interventions they use—her words turn crisp. "I think women overall are sensitive creatures and don't want to offend. We're also in the South, and there are southern niceties that exist that are bull crap. Time and time again, I've heard women say, 'I don't want to change doctors because what if my doctor is upset?'"

Nicolle raises her eyebrows. "Really? What about *you* being upset? What about you actually being in danger because of the way your doctor practices?"

Here, Nicolle pauses, her tone softening. "I think we're by nature sacrificial. We sacrifice for our children. We sacrifice for our husbands. And that goes into birth. We're like: *Okay. I can make it happen. I'll make it work. It will be fine. This is just a woman's plight.* Or women will turn their care over to their husbands, and the husband is afraid of losing her and feels safest in a hospital with a doctor, and so women abdicate their responsibilities to their spouses, to the patriarchal system that exists."

I nod, recognizing in an uncomfortable way how often I've done exactly what Nicolle has described. *It will be fine. I'll make it work.* In fact, the only reason I hadn't pursued a home birth and

contacted Kim when I was pregnant with my son was because of
my husband: he did not trust that I would be okay outside of a
hospital setting. As I listen, the accuracy of Nicolle's statement
digs beneath my rib cage, and yet something about her comment
piques my curiosity, too.

When I moved to Arkansas, I was troubled to hear that the
local public high school sponsored after-hours Bible studies and
a beauty pageant for its young women. I was also deeply troubled
to discover that the local community education program offered
twice as many activities for boys as for girls. When my daughter turned four and all her friends began attending gymnastics
classes, the only place I could enroll her was Sonshine Academy.
Son, of course, in reference to Jesus.

In such a culture, what does feminism look like? Nicolle uses
the word "patriarchal," and she speaks of her work as a means
of empowering women—all things I would associate completely
with feminism. Yet she also distances herself from reproductive
justice movements and firmly roots herself in the evangelical
church.

When I ask how she would describe herself in the context of
feminism, Nicolle sits back in her chair, surprised. It's clearly not
something she's been asked before. She smiles slightly, seemingly
pleased by the question. Then, slowly and measuredly—though
with just as much enthusiasm as before—she works her way
through an answer that criticizes misogyny in the world, insists
on the equality of the sexes under God, but also recognizes men
as the head of the household.

"Over my Christian life," she admits, "I've wrestled with that.
Quite honestly, I've wrestled with the ideology of a submissive
woman, especially after moving to the South. Christianity in
California was a little different. Women were still submitting

there, but they were also doing stuff. In Arkansas, women submit and stay home—and there's nothing wrong with staying home—but there's this sense that if my husband tells me I can think, I can think, and if he says I can't, I can't."

Nicolle grimaces, recalling a conversation at her church not long after she and her husband moved. Because she has the kind of personality that fills a room, eclipsing that of her more introverted husband, someone asked, derogatorily, who ran her household, him or Nicolle.

"I was like, *Excuse me? Excuse me?* I was really offended," she says. "He assumed I dominated over [my husband] or something. So that was very challenging for me, and it made me question who I am, and what I am supposed to be, and what is right from a biblical or Christian standpoint. Then I started to see all of these female heroines in scripture, and I thought…I mean, obviously God is the hero of the entire story, and the book is written about him for his glory. At the same time, he's utilizing different people in different places. Why would he choose to use a woman at that time, knowing the culture said the testimony of a woman wasn't valid? Why would he choose to birth through a woman? To me that says, *Baby, you can do this*. Birth is in the realm of all things possible, and it's not broken."

However, despite her firm belief in women's rights—and particularly their rights in matters related to birth—Nicolle didn't attend the 2016 Women's March in Arkansas. Like many evangelicals, she thought it was too connected to abortion rights.

"I'm definitely a thousand percent pro-life, from womb to tomb, whether you are an unborn child, a black male teenager, or a homeless drug addict," she tells me. "Or rather, I'm pro-choice to a degree, but the choice begins when you decide to lay down in bed."

She laughs lightly. "So when you lay down and when you have sex, what comes of that is just what comes, whether a baby or a disease."

Only in cases of rape or incest, she says, would she close her eyes. "But the statistics [of abortion after rape] are very low. So I think it's interesting. I think people are choosing convenience, and I think we're selfish. Women are sacrificial in general, but when we're younger, there's just this selfishness that comes with babies and how your life is going to have to adjust."

Nicolle pauses and looks out the coffee shop's window, toward the gas station, a bank, and Conway's largest grocery store. Then she laughs again, this time uncomfortably. "I don't know, that's a lot. That's a lot."

She pauses a little longer. "Some of it may be inconsistent. I don't have a lockdown on it yet."

Which is true, of course. Yet critiquing women for being too sacrificial and not standing up for their birth choices, but then saying they aren't sacrificial enough if they want an abortion, speaks to the complexities of reproductive rights at this moment in time, and how, for many, the pendulum can swing all too quickly between the two words—sacrifice and selfish—leaving little room for anything else.

On a political spectrum, Kim sits toward the left, closer to the image I carry of a stereotypical birth worker. She speaks of her aunt, an "earth mother" who breastfed her children until they were two or three, and she openly criticizes the cultural pater-nalism that has eroded women's rights, led to the vilification of midwives, and continues to impact the protocols midwives are legally required to follow. "Look at our politicians," she says. "Our politicians can sexually harass and not get kicked out.

They can do these things and keep on trucking, and *these* are our policymakers?"

Yet, when I ask if Kim considers birth a feminist issue, even she does not say yes. Instead, she talks of "human rights and the baby's rights." She says it's about women having autonomy over their bodies, but her emphasis is on the human.

"How are we imprinting on the mothers, the babies?" she asks. "What are their first experiences?" She wants women and babies to feel loved and nurtured in that moment of birth, and she believes enabling and supporting more peaceful experiences could have a significant impact on our culture.

"We are making birth more hectic and traumatic than it should be. We are pushing these babies to be independent and teaching them to cry it out and that they can't trust us. Parents are afraid to spoil their babies and to co-sleep. They wean early. It doesn't have to be like that."

Instead, Kim alludes to research in human development and psychology, which also recognizes how much a child's wellbeing and adult behavior depends on healthy early attachments. In *The Myth of Normal*, Gabor Maté links a lack of touch, attunement, and responsiveness from caregivers with the increasing amounts of physical and mental distress experienced by adults. (He also points out that attuned parenting requires relatively unstressed parents—something hard to come by in a culture that often doesn't offer adequate parental support.)

Although societal constraints exist, and Kim doesn't judge individual parents, she says she'd like to see the entire culture treat each other the way midwives treat mothers and babies—supporting them, nurturing them, helping them to trust themselves and to move through an intense life experience with patience and respect.

"If the majority of people treated one another like this," she says, "our whole society, our whole world, would be in a different place. So it isn't women's rights or human rights, either. It's peace on earth."

Her description pulls me in. A world where respect for life begins at birth—for mothers as well as for infants? Yes, please. Yet neither Kim nor Nicolle calls herself a feminist. Neither will take on the weight of that word.

When I was growing up, I, like many of my Catholic and Lutheran peers, equated feminism with "femi-nazis" and bra burning. At the bus stop or in my bedroom, playing with Barbies and cutting paper dolls out of the Sunday ads, my friends and I would blush when we heard the word, and only repeat it in a whisper. It wasn't until my high school AP literature class that a teacher of mine openly identified as feminist. For the first time, I read Virginia Woolf. I read Annie Dillard. I read Alice Walker and Toni Morrison. Around then, I house-sat for a college professor who had PhDs in theology and computer science and subscribed to *Ms. Magazine*. I'd water her violets and flip through issues while drinking tea on her couch. These, I thought, were women who pursued their professional and artistic goals. Women who knew their minds mattered and did not let cultural expectations for domesticity hold them back. I promised myself I'd become one.

And yet I followed a fairly traditional path. Though I participated in book clubs and the honor society and went to college, and though I valued my education more than my dating life, I struggled against the sexism I saw in the Catholic church and yet yearned for that community. I both desired the stability of family life and feared feeling tied down. Oftentimes, the pull of stability and domesticity won—even though that did not fit what

I thought of as feminism. I did not participate in pro-choice (or pro-life) rallies. I shied away from women's and gender studies classes. My hobbies in college including hiking and biking but also quilting and cooking. My long-term goals included a writing life and a comfortable house. When I met, at a Catholic youth group in college, a partner who valued my intelligence and supported my career goals yet understood the pull of my cultural background, I accepted that path. At the age of twenty-four, I was the first of my high school friends to marry. I had my first child when I was twenty-six.

It wasn't until I moved to Conway, where religion wasn't something you could passively ignore but was magnified and amplified on billboards all around me, that I realized how far from Catholicism I'd strayed.

Yet Catholicism, I was beginning to realize, still followed me, coloring what I thought of feminism, femininity, and motherhood, and whether the three could intertwine.

As I drive away from Kim's office, past the widely spaced ranch-style houses, the Tractor Supply store, the gas stations and tattoo parlors and hair salons and Christian day cares, I wonder why even these otherwise strong advocates of women resist the word "feminism," much like I once had. But I also suspect I know the answer. Arkansas is a state where a group of Boy Scouts stared distrustfully at the words "Wild Feminist" screen-printed across my friend's T-shirt. A state where, in 2016, one of my brightest, most thoughtful female students wrote two essays: one that mourned the presidential loss of Hillary Clinton, and another that mourned the fact that my student, herself, at age twenty-two, had not yet committed her life to a husband in front of her Baptist church.

In this context, Nicolle and Kim's comments make sense. To keep their businesses alive—which they each need to do to make a living—they cannot rely only on "feminist" clients. And thus, to appeal to the large percentage of women who populate Central Arkansas, they must meet women where they are.

The women in Central Arkansas who hire doulas or use a midwife for a home birth can consistently be categorized by three words: "Well-educated white ladies," Kim says.

In fact, even when a white, educated, but same-sex couple calls Kim, they do so hesitantly. Their first question is always whether she is comfortable working with lesbians. "I just feel for them," she says. She suspects many of her lesbian clients choose a home birth primarily to avoid local hospitals, where they can't guarantee tolerant and respectful staff.

Nonetheless, the images on Kim's website depict a very white, hetero, evangelical norm. Blonde and brunette women hold their newborns, their faces glazed with ecstasy, while a husband smiles on. Only one testimony directly references lesbianism, and there are no photographs of women of color.

Up until 2017, Birth by Design's marketing strategy wasn't much different. Nicolle didn't target environmentally conscious yuppies, because, as she states, "they're going to find us." Instead, she targeted "the Christian woman of the South who has babies but doesn't talk about sex. That submissive, subservient woman who feels like this is a 'bad thing.'" These were the people who populated the area—the "bread and butter" she needed to reach in order to grow as a business and change the culture's attitude toward birth.

Today, Nicolle is making it her goal to target minorities. She wants to see more African Americans utilize doula support, and she wants to see their risk factors go down. "I can almost guarantee you that if you're African American, single, and pregnant, the likelihood of you having a caesarean delivery or being induced is high." This troubles her, and she's troubled by the fact that, even as an African American herself, she has very few minority clients. "Maybe its affordability," she says, "but I almost feel like it's not affordability. I almost wonder if, as a people, we're more accustomed to serving rather than being served, and so we don't seek out those things that would serve us. Instead, you have to be tough—*stop crying, just have that baby, Girl*—that's the culture, and that's what's being taught and perpetuated."

In response, Nicolle has begun marketing specifically to women of color, and she's seeking funding that would help her offer a sliding scale for women of color who cannot otherwise afford doula support. She is also speaking out more about disparities in health care. She recently discussed milk sharing on public radio, and she served as a panelist in Little Rock following a showing of *Death by Design*, a documentary that exposes the significantly higher rates of maternal death faced by African Americans.

She's been rewarded with an increase in African American clients—a fact that fills her with joy and has led her to consider midwifery. "I'm scared to death," she says, "because things do happen, and it's a big responsibility, but I feel very tied to reclaiming birth, both as a woman and as an African American woman."

There are currently no African American midwives in Arkansas, and only two African American ob-gyns in Central Arkansas. In potentially joining their forces, Nicolle says she's channeling the "granny midwife" of the nineteenth and twentieth centuries, the woman who, admired for her wisdom, skill, and knowledge of herbs, "held it down and birthed *all* the people."

Though the granny midwife has been forgotten, Nicolle wants to reclaim her.

Listening to her, I want her to reclaim that woman, too.

Near the end of my second pregnancy, I attended one of Nicolle's prenatal dance classes. The classes—designed to position fetuses for birth and help mothers tone the muscles they need during labor—took place in a brightly lit, mirrored dance studio in one of Conway's newer commercial areas. Each week, five other women and I sat on the birth balls Nicolle had placed in the room and rolled our hips. None of us considered ourself a dancer, so we at first giggled and joked. Nonetheless, we followed Nicolle's instructions: wrapping coin skirts around our thick waists and draping neon scarves over our heads. We looked like belly dancers as we did figure eights, swung our hips, and sashayed—movements Nicolle insisted would aid the infant and later ease the pains of labor.

At the end of every class, Nicolle transitioned from upbeat music to a slow, sentimental song about motherhood and guided us through a series of arm motions. We cradled our bellies with our hands, and then pretended to hold and rock an infant as the song moved through its prayer. Nicolle smiled. The other women smiled, as if imagining some perfect serenity, some ideal Madonna and child. As if this experience were beautiful and we were all holy and blessed for going through it.

As I gazed at the other women's faces—the pear-shaped lesbian who flinched as she walked and would end up laboring for twenty-four hours in the hospital she'd wanted to avoid; the thin, snappy mother of four who admitted she grew depressed after the birth of her last child and was now unexpectedly pregnant with her fifth; the pastor's wife, who insisted on a home birth

whether or not her husband agreed; and the woman furthest
along, red-faced and somber, who'd cried at the beginning of the
first class and asked Nicolle to pray for her—I expected they believed it: the holiness, the perfectness, the blessed belly. In their
serene and quiet eyes, I saw an acceptance and faith that I did not
then feel myself.

I have thought back to that moment many times when trying to reconcile my own beliefs about birth and women's bodies
with the evangelical culture that predominates in Conway. I have
often worried that my biases have caused me to too quickly judge
the doctors, doulas, and mothers I meet. The fact that Nicolle's
company is so steeped in evangelical Christianity strikes me on
two levels. First, it shows how much mother-friendly birthing
practices can, and should, transgress political and cultural divides. Mother-friendly birthing is just as necessary in Arkansas
as it is anywhere else. It is just as necessary for these women as
anyone else.

Second, it humbles me and forces me to interrogate my own
assumptions. If much of my critique of birthing practices is a critique of the patriarchy, and if I associate most organized Christian
religions with the patriarchy, does that mean healthy practices
can't also come out of Christian organizations? I admire all that
Nicolle is doing in Central Arkansas—the much-needed services
she offers, her genuine love of and support of birthing mothers,
the awareness she is raising in a culture that is not quick to accept
anything labeled progressive. She is doing things I cannot, and
she is able to reach an audience that I cannot. She is, in fact, able
to reach *many* audiences—the Southern Baptist minister's wife
as well as the lesbian couple who carefully ask which hospitals
they should avoid. She supports them all, through their home
births and their unmedicated hospital births and their epidurals.

She discusses gentle C-sections and helps mothers find agency when complications arise. She makes it clear that she does not judge women for their choices. Nor does she advocate for a "best" way to give birth. Instead, she listens and guides so that women feel empowered no matter what their birth looks like.

In a culture such as ours, which tends to pit women against each other—pro-life versus pro-choice, Christian versus atheist, even mothers versus nonmothers—this kind of advocacy, this kind of listening, is crucial, and perhaps what we need most in order to address not only women's birth options and worsening maternal outcomes but also the country's religious and political divides.

That day at the dance studio, when the women lowered their arms and opened their eyes, their faces shone. Although I did not fully mirror them—I could not then pretend to find a prayer uplifting or share their comfort in Christian motherhood—Nicolle had created an environment in which they felt safe and respected. For a brief moment in Arkansas, our bellies wrapped in coin skirts and reflected on the walls, she offered us peace on earth. "Baby, you can do this," she said. "Birth is not broken."

ON THE SILENCE
OF REGRET

One day this past spring, a few months after I gave birth to my son, a mother stopped me at my daughter's preschool. "You look great," she said. Rather than smile, however, the woman frowned. She was eight months pregnant, retaining water, and clearly uncomfortable. As she shifted in front of me, I wanted to tell her how far from great I felt. My son had slept poorly, and I had spent two hours in the middle of the night slumped in a rocking chair, battling a resentment that left me ragged and exhausted. Yet I did not know how to break through the woman's perception that everything was fine, so we just stood there, silent.

That silence wasn't an unusual occurrence. Indeed, I'm endlessly surprised by how hard it is to talk about the complexities of motherhood with other mothers. Everyone's stories and experiences are different, and you'd think this would validate the need to talk more, and more often, and to disseminate and distribute a wider array of stories. Instead, we silence ourselves, wary of offending others for the choices they have made, wary of revealing our vulnerabilities and doubts to someone who might judge us against the impossible cultural ideal—a woman who sheds the baby weight easily, is never self-conscious, and even in the midst of sleepless nights will look at an infant's tiny features and melt into a puddle of joy. The ideal is unrealistic, of course, but that does not stop us from using it as a ruler.

For instance, I married my college boyfriend and had my first child when I was twenty-six, not altogether unusual for a white middle-class woman who grew up Catholic and went to college. However, I am also an academic mother, and thus I am surrounded by women who either choose not to have children or who carefully plan them around graduate school and tenure, sometimes waiting so long that they encounter issues with fertility. As a result, babies in this group tend to be deeply, deeply wanted, and these highly educated women tend to be fairly obsessed, researching and interrogating childbirth practices, hiring doulas, and committing to attachment parenting. Indeed, the women I know who breastfeed long-term are either stay-at-home moms or academic mothers, likely because the two groups have more in common than we often think. They both do things fully. All the way in. They are 100 percent committed.

In some ways, I contribute to this stereotype. I deeply, deeply wanted my daughter. I read everything about birth practices, breastfed for twenty-seven months, and only fed her organic, homemade baby food. In other ways I'm an anomaly. My older child may have been deeply wanted, but my younger child resulted from an unplanned pregnancy. I did not, actually, want to be pregnant, and in light of that fact, it is very easy to judge myself according to how I perceive these other academic women— women who are driven and who have claimed control of their bodies and their careers—and to feel belittled and less than perfect in comparison, because if I really had claimed control of my body and my future, I would still only have one child.

Such regret, it turns out, is difficult to discuss. A few months ago, I attended a writing conference designed to encourage and support women writers in a field that still privileges the work of men. One of the panels discussed how to balance motherhood and writing, and when someone asked the panelists if they ever resented their children for taking time away from their writing, each of the panelists quickly said, "No, of course not!" almost aghast, as if that were the strangest question. The room promptly fell into silence.

At the time, I was still nursing my son, my breasts were full, and soon enough I'd carry my breast pump in its black bag to the single-stall bathroom, where I'd sit self-consciously for fifteen minutes, shivering in the draft from the high window, listening to the pump's conspicuous beeping, and cringing each time another attendee tested the doorknob. I resented having to pump in that bathroom, having to pump in many awkward bathrooms. When I longed to read and write but couldn't because my children were young and needed me, I sometimes—no, let's be honest, I often—resented those caretaking tasks and the time they required. It's not that I resented my children themselves—their individualities, the smell of sweat in their hair, their knobby knees and pursed lips—but rather the time child-rearing took away from other things I loved to do, things I loved to do sometimes more than supervising my kids, and thus I sometimes wondered if I should have made different choices.

I wanted to ask those panelists, those women writers who sat in the front of the room and admitted to struggling to find time to write, to tell me about their darkest moments, the moments they longed to write but couldn't. The moments a book, or a project, or a life goal felt just beyond their reach because they had to go to the grocery store or tend to a vomiting child. "In those moments," I wanted to ask, "do you ever miss the time you once had? Do you ever feel it was too much of a sacrifice? Do you ever regret having children?" But I didn't, which now strikes me as unfortunate, because is that really such a terrible or even uncommon thought? To sometimes feel lost? To accept that sometimes parents do indeed feel regret?

I was still thinking about these questions a few months later when I took my daughter to the public library in order to waste time. It was the end of her winter break, and I had run out of ways to entertain her. What I *really* wanted was to be alone. To work on an essay and read by myself. Instead, I read her children's books and followed her around and pretended to eat plastic pizza off of a plastic plate in the play area, and then I sat next to her at the preschool computers while she clicked through a series of letter and number games. A large bright sign reminded me not to leave her unattended. The adult section was across the building. I didn't want to spend all day on my phone, so I just sat there people watching, and for a long time the only other adult in the room was a mother about my age with four young girls. The woman, unlike me, had clearly spent time that morning straightening her hair and putting on makeup, and she appeared a whole lot more content than I felt as her four young girls pranced through the area, placing copious amounts of library books in the gigantic canvas bag she'd brought for the occasion. The mother seemed happy. I expected she was probably never, ever plagued with resentment or regret.

After I wallowed in self-pity for a while, wondering, for a brief moment, if my own children would be better off with a mother like her, the well-groomed mother of four told her children it was time to leave. They fussed a bit, begging to stay longer, and the woman raised her voice when the second youngest tore off.

The woman sighed, defeated. "I'm so, so sorry for the noise," she said as she passed me, and the entire situation suddenly struck me as absurd.

Maybe that mother was content at the library that day, but maybe she wasn't. Just like I am sometimes content to watch my children play, while other times I yearn for a distraction. Yes, it would be nice if I were always involved—if all parents were always blissfully involved—but involvement twenty-four hours a day, seven days a week, is a pretty high expectation, and in the long run not all that healthy for the children. Why are we holding ourselves to such high expectations? Pretending that we love it, 100 percent, when to be honest, a child is a child, a lot of fun, yes, but also a lot of work, very little of it uncomplicated. Indeed, I find it quite ironic that we accept a whole lot of complexity—including resentment and regret—in relationships between parents and older children but not between parents and elementary kids or infants. When my siblings and I were in middle school, my mother proudly wore a T-shirt that read, "Mothers of teenagers know why some animals eat their young." It usually brought a knowing laugh. Teenagers and young adults can be a challenge; we accept this as life.

Or *perhaps* we do. I once took a poetry workshop with a woman who encouraged us to "enter the cave" and write about the fears and memories that scared us. She'd give us a prompt, send us out of the room, and we'd reconvene in a half hour to share, unedited, what we had written. The workshop leader would read what she wrote as well, and her own poems tended to explore her relationships with her adult children, including her son, someone who had disappointed her by turning conservative and adopting a corporate lifestyle. The poems dripped with regret, conflict, and grief. It was clear that, though she loved the male child who once clung to her nightgown, she didn't entirely love who her son had become.

What I remember most about that experience is the uneasy glances passed between a few other students and me as she read. We felt embarrassed listening to her, not because we didn't trust the authenticity of her feelings but because her feelings did not affirm the world as it should be. *How could a mother not love her son? What did she do wrong?*

It embarrasses me now to think about that judgment—the way we so quickly turned to blame her as a parent, as if her in-attentiveness was the cause of her son's distancing, but also the way we so quickly moved to silence *her*, to critique her decision to write about her son in those ways. *Why would she do that? What would he think? She's ruining any chance of reconciliation*, we whispered to each other after class. I know now that we were young and naïve, yet in silencing her we nonetheless enforced patriarchal ideals. When her story did not present a mother as nurturing, self-sacrificing, and capable of unconditional love—everything we'd been taught to value—we censored her.

I recently read Rebecca Solnit's book *The Mother of All Questions*, which includes an extended meditation on the politics of silence. "Silence," Solnit writes, "is what allows people to suffer without recourse, what allows hypocrisies and lies to grow and flourish, crimes to go unpunished. If our voices are essential aspects of our humanity, to be rendered voiceless is to be dehumanized or excluded from one's humanity. And the history of silence is central to women's history." In a compelling—and sometimes overwhelming—case, Solnit lists the many ways women have been silenced as a result of the patriarchy, from the ways most religions and courts have historically denied women a voice, to the way medical studies continue to examine PTSD primarily in war veterans rather than victims of sexual abuse, even though rape causes PTSD far more often. One of Solnit's responses to such silencing is to validate women's stories and the telling of women's stories, in all shapes and forms:

> We are our stories, stories that can be both prison and the crowbar to break open the door of that prison; we make stories to save ourselves or to trap ourselves or others, stories that lift us up or smash us against the stone wall of our own limits and fears. Liberation is always in part a storytelling process: breaking stories, breaking silences, making new stories. A free person tells her own story. A valued person lives in a society in which her story has a place.

Interestingly enough, the complexity of motherhood is one of the subjects women aren't particularly encouraged to explore. Though women, over time, have given themselves permission to write about a great many issues, many still hesitate to write about motherhood or their children. In an editorial published in the *Los Angeles Times*, Sarah Menkedick discusses her initial tendency to "apologize" for writing about motherhood. "Patriarchal culture," she observes, "has reduced motherhood to an exercise no serious artist would tackle as a subject." Other female writers cite their children's privacy as the reason they avoid the subject. At a conference, I once heard a female writer make a convincing argument that writing about her children took away their agency. She said she could write about her ex-lovers, her parents, and her friends because they were adults, perfectly capable of writing back if they disagreed with her presentation. Her school-aged children, on the other hand, could not. She didn't feel like she could infringe on her children's privacy before they understood the implications of publication and were capable of giving consent.

Plenty has been written about the ethics of writing about others, especially about family, and I agree that we should not write about those we know without carefully considering the implications and consequences. I also understand that many fathers have similar qualms. Scott Russell Sanders once said he wrote about his children when they were very young, but after they became preteens and teenagers, he stopped. He no longer felt like those were his stories to tell. Only when his children were adults, and he could ask for their permission, did he begin again. I admire him for this approach and the thought he put into it, just as I admire each and every female writer for the sometimes uncomfortable decisions she comes to when she chooses what and what not to share about her experience as a parent.

However, I'm also wary of this self-censorship, especially when women, whose stories have been silenced for such a long, long time, remain the primary caregivers even in households with two working parents. What does it mean when a female writer cannot share and describe what could likely have been one of the most transformative experiences of her life? Why are we so afraid to know what mothers think of their children? (If our experiences were only positive, only uplifting, we would not hesitate.) Is it because such stories would remove a veil about motherhood that we as a culture are not ready to confront? The mother who does not and is not willing to sacrifice 100 percent for her children? The mother who perhaps doesn't always like her children? (Can I say it...the mother who sometimes regrets mothering?)

At its core, parenthood is biological. A unique mix of hormones spikes during puberty, developing sexual organs and propelling males and females alike to show an interest in things they hadn't shown an interest in before. We joke about this "teenage sex drive," and when teenage girls claim they never want kids, we often say, "Oh, just wait until you are twenty-five or thirty," in part because many women do, indeed, experience a biological, hormonal desire for children around that age, a desire they may or may not choose to follow. The drive to reproduce and sustain a species is entirely natural, and there are all sorts of hormones involved with pregnancy and child-rearing that help us be loving, form attachments, and thus perpetuate our species.

But if oxytocin and other hormones drive our compulsion to reproduce and love our children, the stresses of caring for those children can trigger cortisol levels that lead to frustration and regret. Both types of emotions are equally natural; they are all embodied responses to our lives on this earth. As a result, we need to stop using their existence as a means of judgment and instead recognize the ways that, from a distance, analyzed across the span of evolution, one mother is actually no different from the rest. Our child-rearing practices may differ, morphing with each decade and generation, but we all birth children, rear them, and raise them. When it comes to generations and eons, our individual significance is dwarfed within the interconnectedness of it all.

I'm tired of thinking that the perfect mother exists out there, and that if I captured enough of those qualities or adopted the right strategies I could ensure a safe journey for my own kids. I can't. I'm also tired of holding myself up to some perfect ideal and letting my failure to meet that ideal silence me. One of the most haunting memoirs about mothers I've read is Terry Tempest Williams's *When Women Were Birds*, which recounts the complicated reaction Williams had on finding that each of her mother's fifty-four journals was blank. Her mother was a matriarch in a Mormon family, a culture in which women traditionally kept journals. In light of that heritage, Williams struggled to understand her mother's decision not to write down her own story, and she struggled to decide whether her mother's silence was a sign of strength and agency or not.

I think of Williams's mother and what regrets those journals might have contained, and I think of a friend's mother, the matriarch of a Catholic family, who had eight children but in her elderly years was wracked with the guilt that she'd contributed unnecessarily to global population growth. I think of the Quaker writer Hannah Whitall Smith, who in 1852 wrote in her diary:

> I am very unhappy now. That trial of my womanhood which to me is so very bitter has come upon me again. When my little Ellie is 2 years old she will have a little sister or brother. And this is the end of all my hopes, my pleasing anticipations, my returning youthful joyousness. Well, it is a woman's lot and I must try to become resigned and bear it in patience and *silence* and not make my home unhappy because I am so. But oh, how hard it is.

We all feel regret. Regret needs to become part of the story. Not something that defines women but something they can admit to without fear of judgment, and thus move through. If I silence my regret, hold it deep in my chest, it burns and it grows, and that is no help to anyone. If other mothers, on the other hand, told me, "yes, I've felt that, too," the regret would lighten and leave, and I perhaps could look at my children in those moments without judging myself as a mother. Because what I'm most interested in, after all, isn't the perfect parent who wanted her children deeply and was enamored with every moment, but the woman who wasn't always enamored yet who cared for and loved her children just the same. Hers, I believe, is the greater story of courage and love. She's the woman who has something to teach me. The woman who I think has something to teach us all.

ON BREAST PUMPS
AND BOVINES

I.

My hatred for the breast pump comes to a head one month shy of my son's first birthday, when the damn thing breaks. I sit in my office, exasperated, as the motor begins to screech and whine and slow and slug—eventually giving out altogether—and I, perhaps like any mother who has lugged her breast pump to and from work for nearly an entire year, and carved out twenty-minute intervals during which to pump milk every two to three hours, and obsessed with not a little anxiety over how much milk she is producing, begin to cry. I shoot off an angry email to the breast pump company, demanding a repair, only to receive a cold, courteous response that my warranty has expired and I will need to purchase a new pump altogether.

That evening, my breasts are so full of milk that it feels like I am carrying two torpedoes, each ready to burst through my skin. My nipples begin to stream before I even lift my shirt for my son, and the milk drenches his face. "It's not funny," I tell my husband, who laughs at our son's closed-eyed squawk. "Really." My breasts ache, and I worry the backed-up milk and now plugged ducts will develop into a case of mastitis—fever, body aches, and all.

The following Monday, a friend saves me, leaning from her car window to surreptitiously hand me her old breast pump in a blue nylon bag. I carry it to my office, and two hours into my workday, I unpack the familiar flanges, tubes, and motor, locking the door. *Thank God*, I think, unbuttoning my cardigan, though once I hold the plastic to my skin, my mood suddenly shifts. I am half-undressed, connected to flanges, which are connected to tubes, which are connected to a motor, which is connected by a three-foot cord to the wall. I am a cow. Merely the provider of breast milk. My worth measured solely by what the pump can extract. My husband can wander his office, the house, his entire life, unencumbered and free. I cannot. I begin to shrink and seethe. I begin to wonder what kind of animal I've become.

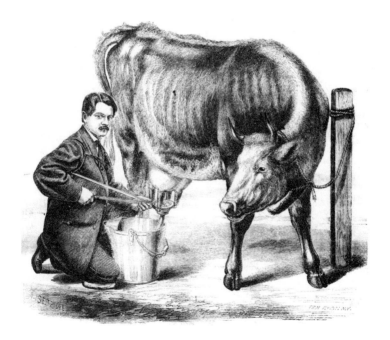

II.

"You know they're basically just milking machines," a colleague whispers a few weeks later after asking if I'm still pumping. Her eyes jump from my chest to my face, back to my chest, and I blush—not so much at her question or her gaze, but at the comparison. I hadn't, actually, equated the breast pump with a milking machine, though I suppose I should have, and when I finally do research the history of breast pumps, the first article I come across isn't about human animals at all. In a January 1864 article, *Scientific American* celebrates the "patent cow-milker," comprised of concave metal pans, india rubber diaphragms, levers, a glass vacuum, valves, and elastic pipe. The greatest achievement: the contraption stays attached to the cow, so the "milkman is free to go anywhere unembarrassed by the instrument."

The issue's cover image depicts a suited man kneeling beside a cow, which is tied to a wooden post and attached to a milker. The cow stands, submissive, and the celebrated cow-milker hangs from her teats, looking a whole lot more like a mechanical parasite with an inescapable bite than an ingenious invention that will gently relieve her mammillary glands. The description beneath the etching informs me—assures me?—that "four elastic thimbles encircl[e] the teats of the cows-udder," but the elastic thimbles look metallic to me. Chafing and uncomfortable, not unlike—as I later learn—the supposedly smooth handblown glass of the era's breast pumps, which would have left a round imprint around each breast much like the imprint left from my own plastic flanges. It takes at least ten minutes for my nipples to shrink back to their original size after the pump's suction has elongated them, and it takes the same amount of time for the red circles to disappear.

I frown at the cow with a great deal of empathy, and then I move on, this time to discover the timeline I've been looking for.

In 1854, Orwell H. Needham submits a patent for the first hand-operated breast pump for nursing mothers. Not long after, Swedish engineer Einar Egnell and Swiss expat Olle Larsson, the founder of Medela, submit patents for the first mechanical pump. In 1874, Robert C. Gray and Charles E. Gassin file a patent for an "improved breast pump." In 1898, Joseph H. Hoover submits a patent for a pump that promises not to "produce pain when the breast is distended."

Joseph H. Hoover is followed by Joseph Lane Hancock (1889), who is followed by Hubert H. Halstead (1903), who is followed by Joel S. Gilbert (1906), Woodard Colby (1926), Erik Lindqvist (1929), Dietrich Von Grolman (1939), and Paul W. Saunders (1945).

The list goes on. Each with bulbs, cylinders, rubber, glass, valves, eventually syringes, cups, and tubes. Each promising something. Less pain. More ease. A simpler design. More "resilient" material. A sensation that will prove "exactly similar" to the sensation of a suckling child.

The images and specifics lose their meaning. All that's important: the list presents an endless convoy of men. Men designing medical devices whose sole goal is to suck the milk from the breasts of lactating women.

Also notable: the number of references that equate breast pumping to milking a cow.

From a 2009 *New Yorker* piece: "Behind closed doors, the nation begins to look like a giant human dairy farm."

From a 2013 *Atlantic* piece: "The earliest versions of the pumps ... were essentially glorified milkers....But male inventors, kindly recognizing that human women are not cows, kept improving on the machines to make them (slightly) more user-friendly."

From the title of a 2016 *New York Times* article: "A Better Breast Pump, Not a Milking Machine."

III.

I feel most like a cow when I pump in the gray stall of a public bathroom, my pump on my knees, squeaking and whirring into the cold fluorescent tiled room. Although I always hope that I'll find myself alone, or that the gushing of sinks will drown out the motor's sound, that usually doesn't happen. "Is that a breast pump? Am I hearing a breast pump?" a woman once said over the stall at a coffee shop, in a tone as high-pitched and condescending as the two undergraduates who cringed at a public university and asked, "What's that *noise?*"

I am not alone in my discomfort. In 2014, Catherine D'Ignazio, a grad student at MIT, grew so frustrated with her breast pump and her experience pumping in campus bathrooms that she and a few colleagues organized the "Make the Breast Pump Not Suck" hackathon. The hackathon, which sought not to just improve the breast pump but to reimagine it, attracted more than 150 inventors, designers, programmers, and engineers.

A few of the pumps introduced at the hackathon or shortly after include the Smart Pump by Naya Health, the Willow, and the Babyation pump. All three originated within households where a career-driven, working mother grew frustrated with her pump and vented to her engineer husband, who thought he could design something better.

I spend an afternoon perusing articles about all three breast pumps, none of which I've previously heard about. Naya's Smart Pump uses water and soft silicone flanges to create a gentler, fluid compression and suction compared to the pull and plastic of traditional pumps. The Babyation advertises soft low-profile breast shields and tubes that don't require mothers to undress in order to use them. The Willow creates a system that's hardly visible when in use. Everything, including the motor, fits in a half-teardrop-shaped contraption that nestles inside the user's bra. On the Willow's website, women pump while holding their kids, taking conference calls, jogging with an infant stroller, and even eating dinner. Only a small glimpse of the white pump peaks out of the cleavage lines of their shirts. Though I expect the pump adds more than a few cup sizes to their busts—more than enough to be "discrete" as the advertisement brags—the women seem happy and mobile and, yes, certainly less tied down than they do in images of other breast pump models.

Many of the articles praise the fact that all three designs were partly inspired by women and designed to meet women's needs. The Willow receives particular praise for Naomi Kelman, its female CEO. When I look up its patent, however, I am disappointed to find that the inventors are mostly men. Kelman isn't on the patent, and as a *Huffington Post* article states, the Willow "was dreamed up by two male inventors."

I am similarly disappointed when I research Janica Alvarez, cofounder of Naya Health. Alvarez played a larger role in the design of Naya Health's Smart Pump than Kelman did with the Willow, but unlike Kelman, Alvarez was unable to woo venture capitalists. Recounting her experience, she says investors didn't know how to evaluate breast pumps and "would rely heavily on their wife's opinion." She tried everything to reach them—she changed her presentation techniques, emphasized women's horror stories, shared breastfeeding statistics, and touted the fact that the breastfeeding industry is valued at $1.2 billion. Sometimes, she says, she even sent her husband into board rooms without her, hoping that if he made the presentation alone, the product might prove more appealing to the largely male audience. Unfortunately, it did not. As an article in *Insider* reports, female entrepreneurs only receive 2 percent of all venture funding, and 93 percent of venture capitalists are male. As Alvarez reports, because pumps are "unique to women and children," they are "not a sexy topic to many."

"As you look at so many common products that we use every day—be it coffee makers or cars—everything else around us is evolving every day. But the one product that is arguably the most important to the nutrition and health of a child is not evolving," she adds.

IV.

I am, I admit, a bit of a sucker when it comes to arguments based on evolution. Tell me that evolution and human adaptation—slowly and magically shaped over centuries—led my body to develop mammillary glands that somehow, incredibly, produce the exact nutrients an infant needs in its first year of life, and that my body adjusts the fat content of milk based on that individual infant's needs and even provides it with antibodies based on the viruses my environment has led my own body to experience—and I will sign up wholeheartedly. The fact that breastfeeding releases oxytocin, of course, doesn't hurt. I can honestly say I generally enjoyed breastfeeding—the quietness of the moment, as my child swallowed large gulps and stared in wonder at my face, and as I stared at his. His mouth was an O on my nipple, a faint tug, a calm pressure.

But I also valued my career and, like many women, needed to work outside of the home. If the world fit my ideal, my workplace would have had on-site day care and I could have simply walked across campus every two to three hours to rock and nurse my child. Unfortunately, such an arrangement did not exist, and I resorted to the pump.

Nonetheless, I cannot recall a single moment when I enjoyed pumping. I have never relished pressing the flanges to my breasts and turning the dial. Nor do I have fond memories of the many rooms in which I committed that act: my own office, with the blinds carefully closed. The bathrooms in movie theaters and office buildings and airports and coffee shops. A make-do "lactation room" at a conference, where the other women and I pretended to ignore each other as each of our pumps beeped in rhythm.

G. B. CRAMP.
ELECTRIC VACUUM MILKING MACHINE.
APPLICATION FILED JUNE 17, 1909.

952,978.

Patented Mar. 22, 1910.
4 SHEETS—SHEET 1.

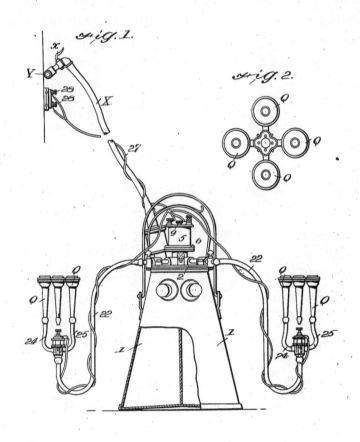

Fig. 1.

Fig. 2.

Now, having researched newer models, I can't help but ask myself if I would have enjoyed breast pumping more with a different kind of pump. With something more discrete, which I could supposedly have used while on a conference call. Something that wouldn't have necessitated lifting my shirt and balancing a whirring motor on my thighs. I'd like to say yes, but I'm not sure that's true. It would have been less onerous, perhaps. I would have harbored less resentment and discomfort. But would I have enjoyed it? Is breast pumping something I could ever have brought myself to enjoy?

Then I think of the cows.

V.

Much like for women, the first handheld cow milking machine appeared in the mid-1800s, followed closely by the first mechanical pumps, which, though called "uncomfortable and damaging" by *Farmer's Weekly*, offered "a starting point for further developments." Those developments included the "less stressful" pulsator (1895), the surge bucket milking machine (1920s), and the rotolactor, still used by dairy farms today.

The rotolactor, also known as the "dairy parlor," works like a slow-moving carousel. Herds of full-uddered cows board, head in and udder out, as the platform rotates toward a farmhand, who attaches milkers to their teats. The milkers milk away, and by the time the cows have completed their circuit, their udders are empty. "Cows are very calm, have their own space, and seem to enjoy the ride," farm equipment company DeLaval brags in its online manual, while also pointing out that their parlors have the highest "cow throughput per hour."

The goal of all of these technologies, according to the *Journal of Dairy Science*, is to "maximize yield and profit," and the latest invention is no different. First installed commercially in the 1990s, the automatic milking system (AMS) promises "to increase milk production by up to 12 percent" and "decrease labor by as much as 18 percent." With its twenty-four-stall platform and five robotic arms, the AMS can milk up to ninety cows an hour, largely due to its "automatic teat-cleaning and milking cup-attachment process." No longer do farmhands have to touch or attach the cups to tender teats. No longer must they visually check for swelling or other signs of mastitis.

The YouTube video I watch about AMS is nothing short of amazing. Stella the cow meanders into a $200,000 metallic contraption with bright red panels. Once she's inside, the small gate closes and a robotic arm moves beneath her to clean her teats and attach the cups. The cups suck away while a computer screen projects Stella's output. When finished, the robotic arm detaches the cups, the stall opens, and Stella leaves, making room for the next cow.

This all works because the machine lures Stella in with nutrient-rich food—a tactic, I might add, also used for humans. To make the pumping experience more pleasurable, which is another way to say, to facilitate the necessary release of oxytocin, I am supposed to eat a favorite snack while pumping, or perhaps listen to my favorite music, or consider pumping a "break" from my work day and a chance to look adoringly at photos of my children.

These strategies generally succeed—even if I never consider pumping a pleasant break. That said, as I watch Stella experience her first robotic milking on YouTube (my own teats tingling), it strikes me that cows do not have smartphones or photos of calves. They are not even lactating for their calves, which are taken away from them shortly after birth to maximize milk for human consumption. The cows are simply there, used by corporations only minimally concerned with the *Journal of Dairy Science*'s warnings that "pre-milking teat preparation" may not adequately "stimulate milk ejection." Or that cup attachment may correlate with increased "kick steps," the mark of cow discomfort. Or that automation may lead to decreases in detection of mastitis, an illness which—in addition to causing excruciating pain for the cow—could spoil the milk.

VI.

When discharging me from the hospital after the birth of my son, my nurse handed me, along with brochures on SIDS, car seat safety, and immunizations, a paper with instructions on hand expression. In other words, how to pump myself using only my thumb and fingers. Although I'd hand expressed a few times while nursing my daughter—usually because I'd forgotten my pump or it ran out of batteries—I'd never before seen such detailed instructions. The paper was filled with step-by-step guidelines for something I'd previously done intuitively, and it included large photos of a woman's hand cupped like a C around her nipple. My husband paused at the images, surprised. I did, too. Rarely does one see such large images of nipples in a context that isn't purposefully pornographic.

At the time, I couldn't bring myself to study the photographs further, though I did store the sheet in a brown folder on my desk, the same folder where, months later, I placed a copy of the Willow's patent. When I take both out now, I marvel at the differences.

Unlike the sheet on hand expression, the Willow's eighty-page patent includes no images of breasts or nipples, even though the pump requires the existence of both. Instead, the patent

U.S. Patent   Jan. 10, 2017   Sheet 1 of 51   US 9,539,377 B2

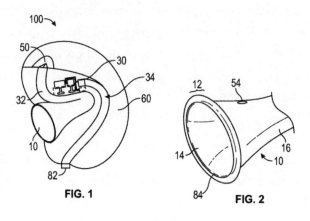

FIG. 1   FIG. 2

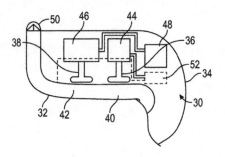

showcases a kidney bean–like diagram with numbers and arrows, another diagram with squares and rectangles, and another diagram of a convex vortex. The attached flow chart asks, "Has pressure dropped to indicate a predetermined volume extracted or predetermined time elapsed?" "Has sufficient vacuum been achieved to establish seal?"

Then a directive: "Operate compression elements to expulse

milk downstream of compression elements." "Contact compliant region of breast adapter to breast."

The language is technical and electric—nothing motherly or nurturing here—and it reminds me of traveling through the airport, where my breast pump is treated like a bomb. Conspiratorially concealed in a black bag in my backpack, my breast pump raises eyebrows and makes TSA agents push buttons and pull on gloves. It requires a revelation, followed by swabbing—flanges flailing as the TSA agent rubs white cloth against the yellowing plastic.

The TSA agent has a reason to be wary. Standing on the other side of the cold metal table, a child on my hip, I think my breast pump—or perhaps more accurately, I myself—*is* explosive. And not in a metaphorical way. Not when I am shoeless, with a child clinging to my neckline and pinching my collarbone, a child I somehow have to finagle while repacking the suitcase after the agent says I am clear.

VII.

I redouble my efforts.

I email Willow to ask more about Naomi Kelman's involvement in the design. I get no response.

I check in on Janica Alvarez only to read that Naya Health has had to shut down completely due to lack of funds. Customers who placed orders receive refunds rather than once-praised pumps, and a tech magazine includes Naya Health among its list of "flops."

The only place I find what I'm looking for is eBay, where I discover that some people collect antique breast pumps, and that I could buy one if I wanted. All I need to do is type "breast pump" in the search bar and there they are: models from the mid- and late 1800s, made in Germany or Pennsylvania or Ohio or Great Britain by companies such as Miller or Ingrams or Akron Rubber. The antique breast pumps most readily available have glass flanges and rubber balls at the end that the user would squeeze to produce suction. The descriptions say, "Ball is not hard. Has wear from age." "Blown glass." "Pre-vulcanized rubber."

For a while, I consider ordering one. I could place it on my desk like a trophy—why and of what, I'm not quite sure—yet it would only cost $15 to $40.

In contrast, when I bought my Ameda Truly Yours back in 2013, it cost $150.

My friend's Medela cost $200.

The Smart Pump by Naya Health first retailed for $599.

The Willow sells for around $400.

The Babyation Pump for $450.

Not all of the newest pumps, of course, are covered by health insurance, which means many working mothers could never afford them. Especially the working-class mothers who are already

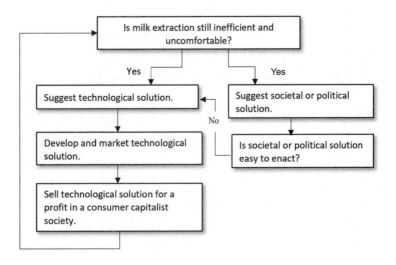

less likely than professional mothers to breastfeed beyond six months.

As for cows, each milking stall in a conventional rotolactor or milking parlor costs between $4,000 and $15,000. Each single-stall AMS costs $150,000 to $200,000.

I make my own flowchart.

VIII.

My final pumping session takes place in a single-stall public bathroom. The bathroom has an electric outlet, so I at least don't have to rely on the pump's sluggish batteries. But the bathroom also has a mirror, which means I have an unencumbered view of my guarded face, my lifted shirt, the flanges and bottles and cords and motor, all connected to the electric cord plugged into the wall. I can see myself sitting on the toilet, leaning ever so slightly forward, into the pump.

Do I look and feel like a cow? Yes. *Should* I feel like a cow? Maybe. We are both mammals, after all, performing the same biological function. Our bodies not so different when it comes to reproduction and milk.

Maybe the problem isn't the fact that, when tethered to a breast pump, I feel like a cow, but rather the fact that society views feeling like a cow, or using a machine that reminds us of our animal selves, as a shameful, terrible thing. Suddenly, it all makes sense. The history of the breast pump. My slight revulsion at pumping. Even the way I cringe when, after an evening out, my husband finds me pumping in our bedroom. The experience of breast pumping harkens back centuries of harmful, cultural beliefs: that lactating is debasing, and that women, like livestock, can be owned and controlled by corporations or men.

The more I think about it, the angrier I am. Especially, it turns out, for the cows. If my greatest critique of the breast pump is that it makes me feel like a cow, what does that mean? What does that mean for the way I relate to animals and the more-than-human world? What does it mean for the cows themselves: purposefully impregnated once a year and then hooked up to their own modern milking machines, at greater risk of mastitis, no music to listen to, dependent on technology that has evolved even more on efficiency, and even less on user comfort, than the modern breast pump?

Perhaps, I think, we both deserve better.

Perhaps the problem is those around us, who see lactating as a means to an end: breast milk for nursing infants. Fresh milk, butter, and ice cream for people. A society that doesn't, actually, respect and honor the act itself and can so easily depersonalize lactation and nursing with words such as "management" and "automation" and "efficiency" and "expulsion."

I wonder what would happen if we treated cows the way I—as a lactating mother—would like to be treated. I wonder how many kick steps a cow using the Babyation or the Willow would record. I know our dairy farmers would likely never *pay* for a Willow-equivalent for cows—something designed to milk them while they grazed outside, peaceful and untethered—but still. I wonder if the experience would be better. Less fearful, stressful, and apprehensive.

Most importantly, I wonder what would have happened if breast pumps and cow milking machines had been designed by women from the start.

IX.

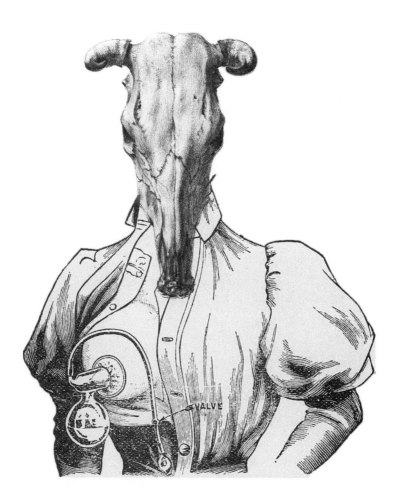

X.

I return my friend's Medela and hold my defunct Ameda in front of the trash can. As sweet-stale smells waft from the bag, I consider the ceremonial. Should I say something? Should I thank the pump—or the universe—for helping me provide milk for my children? Should I shower the pump with gratitude for its beeping and its suction and its loyalty almost until the end?

Should I keep the pump on the top shelf of my closet, as a kind of memento? The once eggshell white but now yellowing motor? The no longer translucent tubing? The small rubbery white valves? Those terribly hard and conical plastic flanges?

Should I honor the pump and what it helped me to do?

I stand in front of the trash can, the pump in my hands, the parts and tubing spilling from my grasp.

I laugh. A single, slight laugh, like the first half of a hiccup. Then I drop the pump in, listen for the thud, and clasp the garbage closed with its child-proof lock.

THE MOTHER-INFANT DYAD

Around the time my second child was born, women began to take breastfeeding selfies—or "brelfies," as they affectionately called them. They'd snap a photo of themselves nursing their infants, overlay the photos with filters and special effects—swirls of deep purples and blues, pastel brush strokes, or washes of vibrant florescence—and post the results on social media. The images, often rendered to obscure the identity of the mother while accentuating the breastfeeding act, were a sign of defiance and pride. In a society where only 25 percent of women breastfeed longer than six months, the brelfies celebrated and normalized breastfeeding by turning the act into art. But when I first saw the posts, what struck me the most was how earthy the images were. Many women added a "tree of life" sticker to their photos, carefully positioning the tree so that the roots covered the woman's breasts, the trunk connected the nipple with the mouth, and the branches of the tree bloomed in the child's cheek. *This is natural. This is what the female body can do*, the images seemed to say. Veined breasts produced milk, which traveled through the nipple, into the child's mouth, propelling growth.

When my son was still very young, I made a brelfie of my own.

One afternoon, I snapped a photo of his small fist on my chest, his mouth on my nipple, and then edited it. I covered my pale bared skin with tree roots. I arranged branches and leaves over his small knit cap. In the background, I speckled the somber wall with pinpricks of light. As my son unlatched and fell asleep—a few droplets of breast milk dribbling down his cheek, the weight of his body settling warm and heavy in my arms—I stared at the photo, willing it to become a celebration. I had breastfed my daughter for twenty-seven months. I was preparing to do the same for my son. Yet as much as I wanted to anoint my experience of breastfeeding as something almost holy—to celebrate breastfeeding as a natural, biological act, an act that efficiently and miraculously offered my child all the nutrients he needed—in the photograph, my face was downturned, my eyes hidden. The air hung more with resignation than peace. This wasn't an image of pride, I realized. It was an uneasy interrogation. An unfinished reckoning with what it means to be female and have a mammalian body.

"We are limited, embodied creatures," Elizabeth Corey writes in "No Happy Harmony." "These limits mean that we cannot do everything to its fullest extent at once, and certain things we may not be able to do at all. The tragic aspect of this is that both excellence and nurture are real, vital goods, and the full pursuit of one often, and perhaps inevitably, forecloses fully pursuing the other."

Corey's "No Happy Harmony" appears in *The Double Bind*, a collection of feminist essays on female ambition. Although the essays in the anthology approach ambition from a variety of angles—sometimes celebrating female ambition as a radical act, sometimes questioning if we as a society should value "ambition" at all—Corey's contribution spoke to me during my

breastfeeding years for the no-nonsense way it addressed physical limitations and motherhood. The drive and ambition one
needs to succeed professionally require extensive energy, as do
nurturing and child-rearing. Women, as a result, may not be able
to "have it all."

When I first became a mother, I thought I could, indeed, have
it all. I was studying environmental writing and preparing to become a professor. Even though I worked at a university where one
instructor told pregnant graduate students to "choose their prior-
ities," I told myself that I could do both things. I could earn my
degree and engage my intellectual self by writing and teaching,
all while simultaneously embracing the mammalian capabilities
of my body. I believed these things naïvely. Hopefully. What I did
not expect is that breastfeeding would push me up against my
limitations, and that these limitations weren't just a choice—me
choosing a priority—but also a biological, embodied fact.

For the twenty-seven months I nursed my daughter, she and I
were both caught in a cycle. As I filled her belly with antibodies
and nutrients that would optimize her growth, I was, simultaneously, flooded with prolactin and oxytocin that caused me to
stare at her softly, to soften at her mouth, and to reach for her at
any hour of the day. We spent long hours on the couch, in the
rocker, or curled alongside each other in bed. In the evenings
those first few months, she sometimes cluster fed for nearly four
hours straight, her mouth slowing as she fell asleep, only to wake
and suck again. I was her comfort, her food source, the one thing
that could quell her cries. And I always came. No matter what I
was doing—whether sleeping, washing dishes, or trying to steal
a few minutes to myself—when she cried, an invisible thread
pulled me toward her. I abandoned dreams, sinks full of suds,
and half-finished books and moved toward her without thought,

lifting my shirt, succumbing to biological processes that ensured the survival of my species.

Yet those biological processes had costs. I needed to drink enough water to stave off the dizzying spin of dehydration. I needed to eat enough food to replace the five hundred calories that lactation required each day. I needed to wear clothing I could easily nurse in, and lift or unbutton that clothing at all hours of the day. The need to be available to her at all times—even when I was sick, congested, battling a stomach virus, or just plain tired and frustrated—sometimes drained me, to the point where I wondered where I ended and she began, where my needs ended and hers began, and whether my own needs and my own mind and body were significant at all.

Bending over her some days as she suckled, I realized that as much as I loved being there, participating in what I believed was my evolutionary, animal self, I also wanted to be somewhere else—and I didn't know what to do with that tension. How could I honor the eco-conscious mother who wanted to do what was best for her child and the earth—who wanted to live, fully, in her animal self—as well as the career-driven women who once swore she wouldn't let anyone or anything prevent her from reaching her goals, yet who found herself, here, bodily tied to another, bending toward a child, serving that child?

As I have done in the past, I turned toward evolutionary biology for answers. For tens of thousands of years, evolutionary biologists say, mothers and infants adapted and evolved in relation to each other to ensure that infants had breast milk. Those adaptations engrained themselves in our genetic code and continue to influence and inform our reproductive and caretaking behaviors. In the scope of human evolution, a mother's role is so tied to her

child's that the two are not discussed as distinct individuals—
mother and child—but rather as a unit: the mother-infant dyad.
The reasons are clear. In the hunter-gatherer populations responsible for that long period of human adaptation and development, mothers carried infants 90 percent of the time, nursed
their infants on demand, and slept alongside their infants. An
infant alone was not safe, so the mothers and infants alike developed behaviors that would promote a close relationship. Infants
learned to cry when left alone, and to quiet when in the hands of
a caretaker. Infants nursed themselves to sleep, and would scoot
toward their sleeping mothers. Infants would respond to touch,
would begin to coo and smile, and if that failed, to flail, thus encouraging mothers to pick them up. Mothers, in turn, developed
a keen sensitivity to the smells and sounds of their infants, and
would wake quickly to stirs and cries. Mothers became hyper
alert, yet when nursing, mothers would calm in an oxytocin-rich
hush. In other words, mothers and infants alike adapted to ensure that the mother was almost always available to the infant.

In the United States today, we tend to refer to these behaviors—extended breastfeeding, co-sleeping, nursing to sleep, and
babywearing—as attachment parenting, words whose contem-
poraneity belies the fact that many Indigenous cultures still do all
of these things. In traditional Mayan communities in Guatemala,
infants co-sleep with parents or siblings and nurse on demand.
In the Republic of Congo, Aka infants are carried so often, they
rarely touch the ground until after their first year of life, and
when they cry, they are offered a nipple within three minutes. It
is in Western societies, anthropologists argue, that we've moved
away from such practices—encouraging formula, trying to teach
infants to self-soothe, and placing infants in their own bedroom
rather than a family bed. "There may be 40 to 50 things that

we do that you don't see in indigenous cultures," anthropologist
David Lancy has reported to NPR, and many of these differences surround the mother-infant dyad.

When I was breastfeeding my daughter, I found myself—
without necessarily intending it—nursing her to sleep for the
first two years of her life. Though most parenting books and even
my pediatrician told me not to—warned me that nursing to sleep
would rot her teeth and prevent her from learning to put herself
to sleep—I did it because it was easy. Because when she was hungry in the evening, and I lifted her into my lap, she simply nursed
for ten minutes and then fell asleep. As breastfeeding women
have known for eons, nursing was the quickest and smoothest
way to transition her into nighttime. So I continued. I nursed her
to sleep at night, and also during naps, sometimes holding her
for two to three hours in the late morning and afternoon, because
only in my arms, my body against hers, would she sleep longer
than thirty minutes.

Yet, in our culture, where I expected my husband and me to
co-parent equally, this also meant inequity. In the evening, I was
always the one to put her to bed, and at night, I always woke before
my husband. Whether my daughter stirred in the bassinet beside
me, or in the crib across the hall, it was me, not him, who heard
her rustling. I would startle awake, wide-eyed, while my husband
still snored, slack-jawed beside me. As a result, I was always the
one to put her back to sleep, or to elbow my husband and tell him
to do so. And the work of feeding her, and comforting her, and
tending her at night meant I was tired and couldn't always focus
at work. I struggled through student papers and led hazy lessons.
I struggled with unfinished essays and half-finished books. My
professional ambitions wavered and dissipated. I couldn't do both
things at once. My sensitivity to my daughter's sounds, and my

breasts' ability to provide her with quick comfort, seemed to be pushing me toward a mode of parenting that eclipsed other ways of life. I would be lying if I said I did not grow resentful.

It is perhaps not a surprise, as a result, that when I found myself pregnant with a second child, my ongoing qualms about my ability to sustain both a child and a career coalesced around feeding choices. The job I held did not offer the same flexibility I'd experienced with my daughter, and I worried I wouldn't be able to tend my son to the degree I'd tended her. As my pregnancy progressed, my memories of the difficulty, unevenness, and unfairness of caretaking began to weigh on me so much a mentor suggested I not breastfeed at all.

The suggestion made sense from a practical perspective: if breastfeeding tied me down, and I grew resentful of my husband when he didn't wake at a child's cries, and I always had to tend her because she was thirsty, why not use formula instead, which would allow the feeding to be more evenly shared? Why not feed my second child a substitute or at least supplement in order to bypass that particular dilemma altogether? Feminists have often praised formula for its gifts of flexibility and time.

My husband, I know, would have supported formula feeding, and my mother even suggested it too, when after my son's birth I did indeed grow tired and frazzled and resentful of the night feedings, the constant demands, and my inability to escape the house alone for even two hours without carefully planning around his hunger. "Maybe you should start supplementing," my mother said a few weeks after my son's birth upon finding me hunched and listless in the living room, staring longingly out the window while my son suckled from my breast.

Indeed, I know many breastfeeding mothers who supplement

because the stress of pumping at work becomes too much, or they can't quite keep up, or their breasts don't respond well to the pump. I also know plenty of mothers who formula feed all along because of difficulty nursing or lack of interest. I never judged them, yet I couldn't bring myself to make that choice, largely out of a sense of guilt. I had nursed my daughter for so long that I wanted my son to have the same nutrition. I believed in the value of breastfeeding, I wanted to support it culturally, and I knew what it offered. Second, breastfeeding seemed, at points, like the only thing I could give him. I worked forty hours a week and started him in day care at seven weeks. I worried that if I stopped—if I lost those daily doses of oxytocin—we'd lose the bond we had.

And so we plunged back into the kind of early motherhood I'd experienced with my daughter: strange postpartum nights where he woke every two to three hours and I sat up in bed, slouching on pillows, nursing him while my husband fell back asleep next to me, if he'd woken up at all. My breasts grew full and leaked milk from the nipple my son wasn't suckling so that I had to change pajamas every night or change nursing pads at least, my entire body permeated with the smell of breast milk. I was tied to him and he was tied to me and there was no other way, and I succumbed, it seemed, to the clockwork of his needs.

I do not remember these as particularly happy times, though perhaps some women do, but I don't remember them as particularly painful, either. Just demanding and exhausting in the kind of foggy dreamlike state of a memory that is receding, something I do not wish to experience again.

My husband fed my son from a syringe a few times that first month before we introduced a bottle and I returned to work, and then it was me and the breast pump again, a thing I hated and yet lugged with me at least five days a week for an entire year. Often after pumping, my nipples would protrude, hardened, poking my shirt, and it would take a while for them to soften and become less noticeable again. At work, I'd walk to the bathroom and look in the mirror and cringe with embarrassment, and I'd cringe again at the sound of the pump in the hallway, where I knew my colleagues and students could hear it—knew they all had gotten used to my schedule: 9:30 a.m., noon, and then 3 p.m. How strange for someone to know your bodily needs—private made public—and it felt, often, like I was trying to force myself into a place where I did not belong, where my lactating body and protruding nipples didn't belong, and I wanted to hide beneath my desk or go home where I could lounge all day in sweatpants and not have to carefully unbutton and rebutton a shirt.

Those days, I often found myself imagining alternative realities. Sometimes I imagined a world in which breastfeeding was supported—where I could bring my child to work, strap him to my chest, and make copies at the copier while he suckled. No one would bat an eye. They'd simply smile, make sure I had enough water, and perhaps bring me berries.

Other days, I imagined the opposite. What would happen, I thought, if I simply stopped nursing? If I bandaged my chest and turned my back to my son's cries?

"Maybe I shouldn't breastfeed," I began to think as I pumped milk in my office. "Or maybe they're right, and mothers should just stay at home." But I didn't want to quit my job, nor did I want to stop breastfeeding, so I continued, tentatively, grudgingly, defiantly, even after the custodian unlocked my office door to empty the trash can and found me, my pump whirring and both breasts bared.

Not too long ago, I came across James McKenna's chapter "Forget Ye Not the Mother-Infant Dyad," which was published in *Costly and Cute: Helpless Infants and Human Evolution*. I was excited to find the anthology—an entire tome about motherhood and evolutionary biology—and I hoped the book's approach to evolution would explain and validate my own impulses in life. It of course didn't—what book has ever offered a perfect ideology or roadmap for life?—but McKenna's complicated, and at times contentious, case for an evolutionary approach to breastfeeding did reframe my questions.

On the surface level, McKenna's research is simple enough. He describes the United States's response to SIDS, and the ways that our concern over SIDS and the suffocation of the infant has deeply stigmatized the act of co-sleeping, which is now seen as treacherous and irresponsible, despite the fact that co-sleeping while breastfeeding—which he terms breastsleeping—is the evolutionary norm. Most breastfeeding cultures today honor co-sleeping, and hunters and gatherers certainly co-slept. The nearness to the mother allowed the breastfeeding infant to easily obtain nutrients overnight, and it was the safest place for the infant. As McKenna states, breastfeeding mothers are hyperaware of their infants at night. They are not actually going to roll over on top of them and suffocate them. On the contrary, co-sleeping has allowed mothers to respond quickly to the needs of the infant, and to protect them immediately in the case of a threat. The mother-infant dyad is such a profound and powerful force, McKenna says, that 12 percent of the mother and baby's sleep behavior is determined by each other—their bodies mirroring each other as they cycle between deep and light sleep.

I remember reading similar arguments on breastfeeding blogs and in literature published by the La Leche League, and most of the women I met at La Leche League meetings admitted that they ended up co-sleeping at one point or another. They told me they got the most sleep if they co-slept. They didn't need to get in and out of bed multiple times but instead woke lightly, helped the infant latch, and then dozed while their infant suckled back into a milk coma. However, they also made it clear that they did not admit to others that they co-slept. And they *definitely* did not tell their child's pediatrician. "When the pediatrician asks where your child sleeps, say the crib," one woman told me. "Most don't understand, and some might even call child services."

This tension between pediatricians and breastfeeding women is, in large part, what McKenna was hoping to counter through his research. In his article on the mother-infant dyad, he describes speaking at lactation conferences and showing endless series of slides of co-sleeping families around the world in order to provide "a new insight for pediatricians unaware of the extent to which Western assumptions of what constitutes 'normal infant sleep' have been exclusively focused fallaciously on the solitary sleeping, formula- or bottle-fed infant, a form of infant sleep that is historically unique, exceedingly recent, and completely anomalous biologically."

He then argues against the critique that breastsleeping is some sort of fad associated with crunchy mothers by writing, in a lovely bit of a rant, "Rather, breastsleeping is an important human behavior, phylogenetically old, relevant, and fundamental to our species, past and present; and judging from the behavior of contemporary neonates and infants it cannot be overturned or suppressed by recent cultural proclamations such as those made by the American Academy of Pediatrics, which claims that infants should not sleep next to their mothers' bodies."

Although McKenna expected some pushback—the United

States, after all, is critical of co-sleeping, especially when practiced by the urban poor or people of color, and few things elicit
the public's fear and anger as much as a news story about a parent who has rolled onto their child at night—he believed in his
message. He wanted mothers to have the freedom to co-sleep
without castigation. As a result, he was incredibly surprised when
the greatest critique came not from anti-co-sleepers, but from a
feminist.

After his presentation, McKenna recalls visiting the conference's book exhibit, picking up Bernice Hausman's *Mother's
Milk: Breastfeeding Controversies in American Culture*, turning to
a random page, and discovering a critique of the argument he'd
just given. Although McKenna was trying to validate the choices
of breastfeeding and co-sleeping women, Hausman, a professor
of medical humanities at Penn State and Virginia Tech, points
out that his research uses the evolutionary mother-infant dyad
to limit women's choices even more. In other words, an evolutionary argument for breastsleeping implies that because wom-
en's bodies evolved to support this mother-infant dyad, women
should breastfeed long-term and co-sleep. Their bodies, and their
lifestyles as a result, must work wholly toward that end. "Expert
advice seems always to have as its goals, whether inadvertent or
not, control over women's actions as mothers," the article quotes.

The critique led McKenna to rethink the impact of his argument, and to acknowledge that an evolutionary narrative on
parenting "too heavily privileges the unique contributions mothers make, portraying women as without agency and forever con-
strained by a seemingly frozen ancient biological legacy, which
seems by comparison not to have hindered the evolution of male
bodies (or behavior) in the same ways."

It is a tension I continue to struggle with. How do I honor

what my body, due to evolution, can do, without feeling con-
strained by that ability? How do I embrace my body's ability to
breastfeed—to grow and then nourish a child—without feeling
like this act further pushes me into a box that has long been
defined by the patriarchy, which would like to see me primarily
as a mother, and would not acknowledge the ways motherhood
is complicated and that sometimes I don't want to be touched at
all—by a child or a man—and that I deserve that right?

I did co-sleep with my daughter. After she outgrew the bassinet that we kept right next to our bed and we placed her in the
crib in her own bedroom, I'd bring her into our bed after the first
waking, and we spent the rest of the night there. I did this because I hated getting out of bed in the middle of the night to sit,
alone, in her room, rocking her until she had nursed and fallen
back asleep. Sitting upright in her chair fully woke me, to the
point where I could no longer sleep. And I felt incredibly isolated
in her room—the sole human awake in a dark and creaky house.
It was better for me to bring our daughter into our bed where I
could more easily fall back asleep, and where the task of nursing
her did not feel so much like a chore, but rather a relationship.

However, I couldn't bring myself to co-sleep with my son.
Maybe they were just different children, or maybe I was through
with being that available to a child all night. But when we transitioned him to the crib in his own room after he outgrew the same
bassinet, and he cried at night, and I brought him into our bed as
I had my daughter, something in me squirmed and retched. I felt
touched-out. I simply couldn't do it. And so unlike with her, I did
stay in his room, rocking him, until he fell asleep and I returned
him to his crib. And yes, as many Western parenting books predicted, he slept through the night much sooner than my daughter did. And yes, as those same books predicted, he learned how

to put himself back to sleep much sooner than my daughter did. And yes, I am thankful for this, even as I also mourn the fact, in a quiet way, that perhaps he did this because I was not as available to him. I was unwilling to be as available to him.

I breastfed my daughter for just over two years, but in the end I weaned my son at fifteen months. One day, after we were down to one or two sessions, I picked him up, and the feeling of his mouth on my nipple brought a physical repulsion. Something akin to a shot of anger or the shiver before the stomach flu. I'd experienced the same sensation the last day I nursed my daughter, when she seemed to play with my body more than she drank, and as I had with her, I quickly unlatched my son, pressed an arm against my lactating breast, and set him on the floor. I knew I had reached a limit.

I do not regret this choice. That said, when I think back to my experiences breastfeeding my son, something in the top of my chest nonetheless tightens, and I get the sensation, once again, of balancing on a tightrope—of trying, precariously, to sustain both a child and a career. Although mothers are supposed to be sacrificing—to their husbands, to their families, to their children—it can be difficult for a mother, or even just a woman, to give herself permission to put her own needs first and to privilege her physical and mental health or career over the needs of her family. Men are allowed to be career-driven, and we expect that long hours at work have a payoff, even though we critique the idea of the "workaholic." If, on the other hand, a mother's dedication to career borders on workaholism, we condemn her. She is neglecting her children. It's perhaps the greatest and strongest criticism of all.

Breastfeeding is such an odd and complicated practice within this context. In many ways breastfeeding presents the mother as her most motherly. She is nurturing her child, wholly devoted to the caretaking act. Yet we also shun breastfeeding. Only in 2018 did all fifty states legalize breastfeeding in public, and although the Affordable Care Act requires employers to give their employees time and space to pump breast milk, women must often take that time off the clock. Thus, the working woman who breastfeeds is forced to try and hold onto both identities—mother and professional—in a world that continues to think of them as incompatible and diametrically opposed. In a world that asks the mother's body to be invisible—at most an accommodation—and her motherly self to be something she can leave at home. As if she could breastfeed and *not* partake in the mother-infant dyad. As if she weren't always ten thousand years of evolution, synapses streaming in an animal self.

Furthermore, if the working mother fails—whether to breastfeed or to keep up at work—there is judgment. She will be judged for being a less dedicated professional, or she will be judged for not adequately tending to her child, which is why there is so much cultural guilt surrounding the practices of infant feeding. I have friends who greatly, greatly wanted to breastfeed—with a force greater than my own—only to find that it was more difficult than they had expected. The infant had a tongue-tie, or they had difficulty latching in the early weeks, or they experienced issues with milk production due to whatever issue and they moved to using formula instead. Some of these women accepted their choice, but some continued to feel guilty about it years later—speaking in hushed voices, or not saying anything at all.

"We had feeding issues. It was very stressful," a friend once told me. "The biology just didn't work." And I knew she spoke the truth—feeding issues in those early postpartum days can be difficult and debilitating, and our culture does not often provide the breastfeeding support that would allow many women to overcome these struggles. And in some cases, some women actually can't. Evolution and biology do not always create perfect specimens. It would be wrong to believe that anything is inherently easy or functional just because it is biological.

Nevertheless, if we continue to see breastfeeding as merely an individual choice that must be made and negotiated behind closed postpartum doors, we are missing the larger picture. Maybe evolution *did* result in mothers whose bodies were biologically adapted to nurture and prioritize the growth of the child—dissolving the mother's own body fat to provide nutrients for a child, and producing a sustaining food source even in times of drought or starvation. But these hunter-gatherer mothers were not simply and solely mothers. Those women still did other things and completed other tasks, and they lived in close-knit communities where the kind of attention and energy that breastfeeding required, as McKenna also acknowledges, was only possible because "of other hominid adaptations, specifically the rise and coevolution of allomothering and sharing food."

In other words, other women and men helped tend the young during the day and provided the breastfeeding mother food so that she didn't have to gather it herself. She was not required to nurse all night and then to hunt and gather her own food. She was not even the primary caretaker during the day. She strapped the child to her back, or others strapped the child to their back, and they went about their tasks. She wasn't simply cooing over her baby all day long. And she certainly wasn't, like me, living five hundred miles away from other kin and working forty-plus hours a week at a job that didn't offer paid maternity leave or on-site day care.

In other words, the "intense dyadic relationship" that McKenna describes, and that continues to affect mother and infant behavior, including my own, did not evolve within our own individualistic culture, but rather in a culture that depended on intense cooperation within a community—cooperation from fathers, grandparents, aunts, uncles, cousins, siblings, and friends. The support of these alloparents was crucial to the mother-infant dyad. Without alloparent cooperation, the biology would not have evolved as it did. Yet, as John R. Gillis argues in *The World of Their Own Making*, and as Michaeleen Doucleff reports for NPR, Western culture has spent the past few centuries devaluing alloparents and often eliminating them from the parenting equation. Few parents can rely on grandparents for extensive childcare, and the childcare industry itself is overlooked and underpaid.

Even more: in the void, the tasks that alloparents once fulfilled—feeding other children, maintaining order in the house, keeping children entertained—have fallen more and more on mothers themselves. Although fathers have picked up seven hours a week of parenting tasks, working heterosexual mothers still spend fourteen hours a week on childcare duties—twice the amount of their parenting coparts. The result: mothers have taken on more and more of the "work" of parenting, and they are completing this work in increasingly isolated and alienated environments. As Lancy concludes, we've created a "mom in the box." And as Gillis writes, "Never have mothers been so burdened by motherhood."

No wonder I, like so many women, took a brelfie during those early months of my son's life. I needed to assert my animal self and to remind myself of all we've forgotten.

Today, when I see a woman breastfeeding at the park, or breast-feeding in a restaurant, or carrying a breast pump through the hallways of an airport or office, I almost recoil. So much of me wants to celebrate her—to celebrate the female body and the miraculous work it does to sustain human life. However, I still, even now, can't quite get to that point, not because I judge her or the act of breastfeeding but because the image of that woman hunched with a nursing cover or scrambling for a private place to pump reminds me of how hard breastfeeding sometimes was, the challenges and demands, and how it made me vulnerable in a way I didn't want to be vulnerable—aware of my body in a way I didn't want to be aware.

"Breastfeeding represents, more than pregnancy, women's heavier reproductive burden," Bernice Hausman writes in *Mother's Milk*. The truth of her statement haunts and constrains me, like a chain—or a baby—you can't quite unlatch. Yet, as Hausman goes on to say, the biological costs of breastfeeding aren't, or at least shouldn't be, the be-all and end-all. Biology isn't the same as scientific misogyny, and a scientific truth doesn't have to be politically or culturally limiting. "If the particularity of mammalian sexual difference confers on women a greater biological burden in reproduction, we can choose to ensure that maternity does not hurt women's participating in civil society and the waged labor market; in other words, we can work to ensure that support for breastfeeding does not suggest the need to cloister women among themselves in the home."

I am trying, now, to imagine what that might look like. I am closing my eyes to envision a different kind of life. I am mostly failing—I have so few models for what Hausman calls feminist evolutionism—and yet I am trying. A culture in which breast-feeding isn't something one has to squeeze into a wage-earning

life. A society in which breasts themselves—growing and shrink-
ing, occasionally leaking—don't draw the kind of attention one
doesn't want to have. A society in which breastfeeding has value
in practice, not just theory, and those around me—my family
and tribe—work with hardly a thought to support the biological
processes of the body. A society in which, for those years I am
part of a mother-infant dyad, my mammary glands are tree roots,
connecting me to a child, but I remain grounded, grounded,
grounded.

ON RACE AND
MOTHERHOOD IN AMERICA

I am sitting in an apartment in the Riverwest district of Milwaukee, the most segregated city in the United States. The location is somewhat arbitrary—simply a quiet writing retreat while my husband visits in-laws across town—and yet here I am, in the top floor of a historic bungalow, one of two original homes on a circle otherwise filled with long, thin apartment complexes, their balconies lit for Christmas or cluttered with old folding chairs. Yesterday, when I walked to the nearest food co-op, I passed an organic nursery, a community garden, a few bars, a soup kitchen, and a park with scarves and bags of mittens tied around the trees. "Riverwest isn't always very safe. Be careful," one of my in-laws told me when I had said where I was going. For a moment I had second-guessed my trip. Then I remembered that "not safe," from a white person, usually means, "not white."

This is the scene I have come here to describe: a few days after the birth of my son, my doula, a Black woman, knelt on the floor in front of me, applying baking soda, hydrogen peroxide, and dish soap to the blood-stained carpet in our master bedroom.

She knelt on the floor on her hands and knees, dipping the washcloth into a bowl of hot water, dabbing the afterbirth, while I—white—sat on the bed, above her.

Though the reasons I did not join her on the floor are understandable—I had just given birth, and my swollen, stitched perineum bled each time I moved—the discomfort of the moment did not escape me. We were in Arkansas, and a white woman was reclining in bed while a Black woman scrubbed her afterbirth from the floor.

A few facts: I grew up in Minnesota, in a white suburban neighborhood followed by a mostly white college town surrounded by farmland. I did not, ever, in my years of education, have an African American teacher. I did not have an African American neighbor until I went to graduate school. I do not remember reading picture books about African American figures, save a few about Martin Luther King Jr. and one with grainy images of two princesses in Africa, and I do not remember watching any shows or movies that featured African American characters until the *Cosby Show*, which partly explains why it took five months after moving to Arkansas for me to realize that the city I now lived in, the neighborhoods I passed through, and the institutions I visited had once been segregated—that "Whites Only" signs had once hung above drinking fountains and bathrooms, that Blacks once lived on the east side of Conway, whites on the west, and that these lines were enforced. I mention this time period—five months—because although my experiences and perceptions are not unusual for someone who looks like me, they have repercussions. For five months, I was blind to the very real history of my adopted hometown.

A white woman reclines in bed while a Black woman scrubs her afterbirth from the carpet. The carpet is cream. The bowl of water begins to turn red. The woman scrubbing pauses every now and then to lean back and rest on her knees. "I don't want you doing this by yourself," she instructs the woman in bed, who nods, compliantly. When the woman scrubbing stands up, she reaches a hand for the wall.

When my husband and I discovered I was pregnant with our second child, we realized we would soon outgrow our rented two-bedroom duplex, and because a mortgage on a three-bedroom home cost less per month than rent on a three-bedroom unit, we began to look for a house. "What neighborhoods do you recommend?" I asked my mostly white colleagues. "Which elementary schools are best?"

Though a few said their children had attended the elementary school nearest downtown, the majority recommended the western half of the city—and preferably the *very* western part of the city, comprised primarily of newly constructed, gated communities, with private swimming pools and private playgrounds, all hidden behind five-foot brick walls. Their elementary schools glistened. Their test scores soared. Their poverty level paled compared to other schools in the district. Their students paled, too.

"We were zoned for Ida Burns, but we moved so that the kids could attend Woodrow Cummins," one woman told me. "It's been such a great experience," she added. "You really do have to think about the schools."

My husband and I do think about the schools. We have long conversations about the schools. We want our kids to go to good schools, but we also want them to grow up within their diverse community, and when we find a house that we like, not in west Conway, but south Conway, a more racially and economically mixed part of the city, schools appear on both sides of the pro-con list I create.

The truth: the neighborhood I am writing this from in Milwaukee does not look so different from my husband's childhood home in South Milwaukee. Though Riverwest perhaps contains more homeless and more city bus riders, the architecture is similar: pale brick duplexes, stone bungalows, and old churches. What distinguishes the two is the people. When I walked to the food co-op yesterday, I saw white millennials in skinny jeans walking home from work, African Americans waiting for a bus, and an older couple looking for a table in the tiny café that served kale salad and three-bean soup. I saw peace poles in front gardens and lawn signs stating "Black Lives Matter" or "I pledge to grow more food." This, in contrast to South Milwaukee, a blue-collar manufacturing town that is mostly working class and white. Walking around my husband's old neighborhood, I've seen signs for parochial schools but never a Black Lives Matter sign or a pledge to grow more food.

The truth: on my walk to the food co-op yesterday, I was pleased to see the urban gardens and the Black Lives Matter signs and the peace poles, but when I passed the park with the scarves and mittens tied in plastic bags around trees, and the sign for the soup kitchen, and the barred bars, and the bus stops filled with grizzled, gray men and tired African American commuters, I recalled my in-law's comment and wondered if I was safe.

The truth: there is a lot I am afraid of and blind to. There is a lot that I overlook.

My doula was scrubbing my afterbirth from the floor because my son was unintentionally born at home—an accidental, unintentional home birth to complement his accidental, unintentional conception. I can recall the sharp terror I felt when the pregnancy test turned positive, and I can recall the adrenaline rush when my water broke next to our bed, and my son's head pressed against and tore my perineum, and I realized we were not going to make it to the hospital.

I can also recall my doula's comment after the first responders arrived and carried me and the newborn on a stretcher down our steep driveway to the ambulance. We had purchased the house in south Conway just two months before, and neighbors we had not yet had the chance to meet—African American on one side, Caucasian on the other—came out of their homes in the early morning to watch the flashing lights and my body swaying on the stretcher.

"Those were really great first responders," my doula said. "They were respectful. Not all are like that."

My doula posts a photo of the first responders on her social media page and praises their work. In the photo, three white men, dressed in full firefighter gear, smile into the camera from the cul-de-sac of our new home. The photograph gets nearly three hundred "likes"—more, my doula tells me, than any other photo she's posted. She looks perplexed when she says this, almost as if she can't quite understand why this, of all her photographs, elicited that kind of response.

When the first responders arrived at our house after the baby had been born, they found me sitting on a towel in the bedroom, wrapped in my husband's bathrobe, holding my son. My son was still attached to the umbilical cord, which was attached to the placenta, which lay in a plastic bowl beside me. The first responders took our vitals and cut the umbilical cord, and when my son began to root, they left the bedroom and stood in our living room while I nursed him. This, I suspect, is what my doula meant when she said they were respectful. They did not rush us to the hospital, or act, in any way, as if I were inept. Instead, they waited while I nursed, looked at our bookshelves, and chatted with my doula about skin-to-skin contact.

I am thankful for the EMTs' discretion and patience, perhaps in the same way they were thankful for my composure. "We didn't know what to expect when we got the call," one of the men told me in the ambulance. There was fear in his voice, as well as relief, which reminded me of a coworker who once gave birth in her bathtub. Uninsured, single, and fairly obese, she had complained of indigestion for months, and when—in her bathtub—the indigestion turned out to be a preterm baby, she went into physical shock. Hers was certainly a different birth scene than mine.

But I also suspect that when my doula said, "They were respectful. Not all are like that," she implied something more. This past fall, during the 2018 midterm election, the undeveloped field across from my daughter's elementary school erupted with Republican political signs. Two weeks before the election, the firefighters added their endorsement, and a "Firefighters Support!" label appeared above the sign for the incumbent state senator, a man who had been cited more than once on Twitter for hate speech against Muslims and people of color. Despite the state senator's angry rhetoric, despite his racist comments—or maybe because of them—he won.

It begs the question: How would the first responders have reacted if I were not clearly middle-class and white? Would they have respected me as much? Would they have trusted me when I said I was fine and when I asked to breastfeed? Would they have given me that space?

I am trying to reimagine my birth. In Conway, all the doctors, physician assistants, and nurses in my ob-gyn clinic were white. All the doctors and nurses I encountered in the hospital were white. One Black woman has written that white doctors consider her "a problem waiting to happen."

If I were Black, and I knew the first responders would consider me a problem waiting to happen, how would I feel, hearing the sirens approach my driveway, those heavy boots stomping into the house?

I have brought with me, to this apartment in Milwaukee, a manila folder with articles about racism and birth. "Nothing Protects Black Women from Dying in Pregnancy and Childbirth," the title of one article from ProPublica and NPR reads. It, like many other articles that have come out in the past year and a half, discusses how Black women are three to four times more likely to die of pregnancy and childbirth than white women—and how the causes go back to institutional racism and unconscious bias. African American women aren't taken as seriously, they have less access to quality prenatal and postpartum care, and they are often forced to work with medical staff who harbor unconscious contempt for Black patients. In addition, they experience chronic health conditions that result from "weathering"—the long, slow wear caused by racial stress. They die from maternal conditions white women are less likely to die from. Even if they are wealthy and educated, they are more likely to die.

I have also brought with me notes from a public panel titled "Informing the Village," during which my doula, Nicolle, sat alongside five other scholars, activists, and health care professionals—all women of color—to discuss the state of Black maternal health in Arkansas. As thunder rumbled and window fans pushed humid air into the room, the conversation kept returning to combativeness:

Black women need to stand up for themselves but are afraid of seeming combative.

African American women, in general, are stereotyped as combative.

If a Black woman asserts herself, by questioning a procedure or requesting clarification, medical professionals call her combative.

Once a Black woman is considered combative, white people treat her differently.

"They'll call security or dope you up," an audience member stated.

After my son was born, I began to feel bouts of rage. My husband and I had proceeded with the unintended pregnancy not because I wanted a second child at that time, or felt it was the right thing to do, but because I did not think my marriage would survive the alternative. In those postpartum days, when my body leaked blood and milk and I was waking every two to three hours at night, I wanted my husband to sacrifice himself the way I had for our family. I wanted him to give up his body—to feel ripped, mauled, and *forced* to give up his body—in the same way I had. The realization that he couldn't—that as a white man in a patriarchal and racist society, he had never been expected to—made me seethe.

"I'm really mad at you, and I don't know how long that will last," I once said. We'd been talking about sexism, and feminism, and household chores, and each time I brought up an inequity in our marriage, he sidestepped, insisting he wasn't a bad person, that he was doing his best, and that I was overexaggerating.

My husband is not a terrible man. He makes my daughter's lunches and carries our son on his shoulders and does so much of the cleaning that I once had to ask him where he stored the vacuum. Yet in that moment, his defensiveness sat between us, a silencing orb, and I realized how often I had swallowed my anger in the face of his discomfort.

These are the conversations I think of when I read Robin DiAngelo's *White Fragility*. In a racist society, DiAngelo states, even progressive whites have been socialized to protect their white privilege. They will twinge with discomfort when discussing race. They will avoid that discomfort by living in mostly white spaces (often for "good schools"). They will insist on their individuality, their independence from history. They will assume the trials and tribulations of nonwhite people don't apply to them. When they hear racist comments, they will say nothing in order to protect the feelings of their white colleagues and friends. They will bristle at any suggestion of white privilege. And if pushed, white women will slump with guilt, or berate themselves with self-blame, while white men will redirect the conversation, draw attention to their own victimhood, or undermine and question the observations and analyses of minorities. In effect: progressive whites will avoid, and thus affirm, racist, societal norms.

I read DiAngelo's book with a combination of fascination, recognition, and horror. Add "sexism" to "racism," and you have my husband, unconsciously shirking whenever our discussions of inequity shine the light on him. But of course, keep the focus on race, and you also have me.

My doula, Nicolle, has begun advocating more and more for Black maternal health. She regularly participates on panels like the one I attended and shares articles like those I've stored in my manila folder. She has worked with other birth workers of color in the state to create a company specifically tailored to protect and empower African American mothers. In the past two years, she has served more women of color than she had in the eight years before.

In response, she has received some pushback. "I have been accused of being divisive in birth work because I've been focusing on the care and treatment of Black women in birth," she writes. She follows this with the Facebook post: "Do not confuse my passion to heal the brokenness in maternity care for Black woman as an effort to be divisive. Maybe take a moment to consider how you may have ignored the harshness of these issues because they don't seem to affect you. To uplift a downtrodden people group is not divisive. To seek to heal or restore what has been damaged is not divisive. It isn't about you."

She of course is right. It isn't about you, which is to say, it isn't about me. And I need to be honest here. I am trying very hard to not make this about me. To not make this about the ways I did—and sometimes still do—ignore the harshness of the issue: the ways, when reading about Black maternal mortality, I have frowned with concern, but pushed the thought aside, believing it didn't affect me, or that it wasn't my issue to deal with, or that I wasn't equipped to deal with it. I have told myself I can write about sexism, and misogynistic politics, and breastfeeding and breast pumps, but no, not racism, this isn't an essay I should write. I have told myself, other voices on race are more important. The voices of women of color are more important. I have told myself, no one needs to know about that moment in my bedroom, when I sat on the bed, and Nicolle knelt on the floor, scrubbing my afterbirth, and I realized this scene had been taking place for generations—very rarely were our roles reversed—and that I was complicit.

I am sitting in Milwaukee, a near-empty coffee cup on the windowsill, papers on maternal mortality spread across the floor. I am sitting here, pausing. Not sure what to do. Soon, I will return to Arkansas, and it will all be there: the house on the cul-de-sac, the drop-offs at my daughter's south Conway school, the field where the firefighters endorsed their conservative candidate, the small red stain that remains of my afterbirth, not on the floor but the wall, more maroon than crimson, but still visible. I will stare at it until the light changes and my breath softens and I get off of my bed.

The truth: Black women die from childbirth three to four times as often as white women. I am a white woman. The numbers bear repeating.

The truth: when I told my husband I was mad at him, and that I didn't know how long that anger would last, he began to listen. He whispered, "I know. That's okay."

The truth: outside my window, joggers pass along the path near the river. The joggers are white. The middle-aged men and young couples, on the other hand, who exit the apartment complex next to me and enter their salt-stained cars are mostly Black. One of the women is pregnant.

The truth: a light snow is falling and I am listening to anger.

ANIMALS ON THE EVE
OF EXTINCTION

Once upon a time, I read my daughter a bedtime story in which dinosaurs and humans coexisted, living together sustainably in cities as well as on farms. They grew crops together, raised young together, and made decisions together. They ate only what they needed and carried no weapons. When they greeted each other and said their goodbyes, they used the phrase, "Breathe deep, seek peace."

For a month each evening, following our reading, my daughter nestled into her pillow, along with sixteen plastic dinosaurs and one plush brachiosaurus, and asked if what happened to the dinosaurs would happen to us. "Will we go extinct?"

For a month each evening, I paused and said: "Maybe. Eventually. But you don't need to worry about that." I kissed her forehead and told her good night, but when I left the room I was still thinking about dinosaurs. I was a mother grazing with my children in a wide open pasture, and when I suddenly looked up, I saw the meteors fall.

EMPEROR PENGUIN • RINGED SEAL • ARCTIC FOX • BELUGA
WHALE • ORANGE CLOWNFISH • KOALA BEAR • LEATHERBACK

TURTLE • FLAMINGO • WOLVERINE • MUSK OX • POLAR BEAR
• HAWAIIAN HONEYCREEPER • BAIRD'S SANDPIPER • IVORY
GULL • WESTERN GLACIER STONEFLY • TUFTED PUFFIN

In my mid-twenties, I began to desire a child. And so I had a child. She was born in a hospital in the middle of December, and she is beautiful, and every day, even when her burgeoning stubbornness forces me to count to ten in my head, her beauty astonishes me. The sharp cut of her jaw. The spark in her eyes. The moles, appearing in greater and greater quantities on her body. She has a zoo of imaginary pets, and she is starting to ask questions about death, and she tells me before bed that she thinks we should all—my husband, me, her, and her baby brother—die together, at the same time, so that we won't be alone. In those moments, when her face opens, asking for something I cannot give, a fear the size of her pupils sears into my chest: that the pain she will experience in her future will not be the pain of a life—of a first love, of love lost, of grief for dying relatives—but a grief so much larger. Lost worlds. Lost lands. Lost species. Lost nations. As the earth destabilizes, as the climate destabilizes, what will her culture become? What will life become? When we are focused so much on adapting, on reacting to the next thing, on wars over resources, what room will there be for joy?

SINAI BATON BLUE • PLICATE ROCKSNAIL • MEKONG
GIANT CATFISH • PHILIPPINE CROCODILE • RESPLENDENT
SHRUBFROG • JAVAN RHINOCEROS • PYGMY HOG •
VARIEGATED SPIDER MONKEY • HAINAN GIBBON • OSGOOD'S
ETHIOPIAN TOAD • TOYAMA'S GROUND GECKO • MARBLED
GECKO

These of course are anxious thoughts. They are the thoughts of
someone occasionally on the brink of despair. The thoughts of a
mother, a parent, late at night. Someone trying to wrest control
over an uncontrollable future. And surely, I think, my fears are
no different than anyone's when the world tips toward instability.
During the Vietnam War, didn't parents fear for their sons? In
Europe and Asia, on the eve of World War II, didn't families fear
for their children? In Sudan and El Salvador, now, doesn't the
bringing of life into the world carry with it a risk that surpasses
the risks of childbirth itself? Only in this case, the threat isn't
nations, or even continents. It covers the planet.

MAGDALENA RIVER TURTLE • TITICACA WATER FROG
• BANAT GRASSHOPPER • PLOUGHSHARE TORTOISE •
MONGOOSE LEMUR • GOLDEN BAMBOO LEMUR • ADRIATIC
STURGEON • RICORD'S ROCK IGUANA • GREAT PALAU TREE
SNAIL • BLACK-BREASTED PUFFLEG • GLAUCOUS MACAW •
GASTLETON'S FLIGHTLESS KATYDID • PARNASSOS GREEK
BUSH-CRICKET • NORTHERN MOSS FROG

Sometimes, out of necessity, I want to turn it all off. I want to
wake up, bring my children to their respective day cares, teach my
students how to write, pick up my children, boil water for pasta,
and toss a green salad. Eat at the table. Play evening games and
then go on a walk. Tuck them in with a bedtime story and a sippy
cup of water. I want those small routines, the comfort of them,
to be everything. I want to not have to think about anything else.
Not: what will this world look like in thirty, forty, fifty years. Not
to know that, by then, 50 percent of the species on the earth right
now will be lost.

WHITE-HEADED VULTURE • HOODED VULTURE • SLENDER-
BILLED CURLEW • CALIFORNIA CONDOR • RAPA FRUIT-
DOVE • SOCIABLE LAPWING • BLUE-EYED GROUND-DOVE
• LESSER ANTILLEAN IGUANA • OKINAWA WOODPECKER •
TAPANULI ORANGUTAN • EASTERN GORILLA • HIMALAYAN
QUAIL

In my son's first year, the US government tried to repeal the
Endangered Species Act. The Clean Air Act. The Clean Water
Act. The White House reduced Bear's Ear National Monument
by 85 percent. They changed the image on the Bureau of Labor
Resources website from a family hiking to a wall of coal. They
filled the cabinet with corporations. They slashed the budget of
the EPA.

On the day of the election, when I was nine months pregnant
with my son, I drove to work in Arkansas. The lawn of Peace
Lutheran Church, next to a designated polling place, was slath-
ered with Trump signs.

TRANSYLVANIAN PLUMP GRASSHOPPER • CANTERBURY
KNOBBLED WEEVIL • THREE FORKS SPRINGSNAIL • BAMBOO
LEMUR • BLACK-AND-WHITE RUFFED LEMUR • LIVINGSTON'S
FLYING FOX • CORAL PINK SAND DUNES TIGER BEETLE •
McCORD'S BOX TURTLE • PAINTED TERRAPIN • HOODED
GREBE

In downtown Little Rock, my daughter runs across the benches
of the Central Arkansas Nature Center, her fingers tracing the
long line of aquariums. "Look, that one has teeth!" she says of the
albino gar, and her joy is great.

Watching her watch the fish, I can't help but imagine the roles reversed. Some alien creature is watching us, a teeming, frothing force of humans, specimens in a vast glass world, and we are coupling. Reproducing. Eating. Desecrating. Taking from the soil. Taking over resources. Like termites, only worse. Or maybe just like termites, only with more tools. Some of us have a god and believe we will be saved. Some of us do not. And it doesn't really matter, but I am just one of them. One specimen, who birthed two more specimens, and from above I move through the routines in my life, and the aliens know what is coming, know the brink my species is bringing itself to, will watch the impending environmental apocalypse, which will not be the end of all life— the earth will remain—but will certainly be the end of a great deal of life, and perhaps even the end of our own.

IBERIAN GREY BUSH-CRICKET • HAWAIIAN CROW • LONG-BILLED FOREST-WARBLER • RED-FRONTED MACAW • NEW CALEDONIAN LORIKEET • YELLOW-BREASTED BUNTING • ORANGE-BELLIED PARROT • CELEBES CRESTED MACAQUE • BLEEDING TOAD • LA GOMERA GIANT LIZARD • CUBAN CROCODILE

Yesterday, it stormed. The sirens went off at 1 p.m. I was at work. My children both at school. I imagined my son's day care teacher rolling all their small cribs against the safest wall in the infant room. I imagined my daughter's preschool, the teachers guiding the students to all make "tents" with their hands beneath the tables. The rain poured down, horizontal. The sky turned green and black. I ached for my children.

That evening, after we all safely returned home, my daughter insisted on a rain walk. She put on her red rain boots and pulled out her children's umbrella. She hopped from foot to foot while I zipped my sweatshirt. Once outside, I lifted my face to the hazy gray sky, and the wind puffed us with its humid breath, and my daughter sloshed through the gutters, the curbs, kicking and skipping through puddles, pointing with delight whenever she saw an even bigger puddle ahead. The neighbors smiled at her and waved—her pleasure in puddles a simple delight for us all— and we slowly made our way halfway around the block. But then the wind picked up, and the sky began to spritz a colder, stinging rain. My daughter's eyes widened. When a gust caught her umbrella, it pulled her forty-pound body backward. "Let's go back inside. Quick. The wind will take us away," she said. Nothing I could say would assure her she was safe.

WHITE-BELLIED HERON • MINI BLUE BEE SHRIMP • RED ORCHID BEE • SMALLTOOTH SAWFISH • BLACK RHINOCEROS • PYGMY THREE-TOED SLOTH • LEAF-SCALED SEA SNAKE • EUROPEAN MINK • FINE STAINED-GLASS LEAFHOPPER • SAN JOSE BUSH RABBIT • SOCORRO DOVE • BAWEAN DEER • IVORY-BILLED WOODPECKER • PURPLE-WINGED GROUND-DOVE • GOLDEN-EYED STICK INSECT • ANGELSHARK

I come from a culture that has shortened the Mississippi River by 150 miles, and for more than fifty years expected labor in hospitals to follow "the Friedman curve." A culture that in its quest for wealth and convenience has mined the mountains and eradicated the prairie and plundered the topsoil until conventional farmers can no longer grow crops without dousing the ground with fertilizer made from oil. A culture that has spewed carbon dioxide into the atmosphere at a rate faster than during previous great extinctions and then hid the facts to protect corporate wealth.

RED-THROATED LORIKEET • KAKAPO • BORNEAN ORANGUTAN
• GIANT IBIS • SIBERIAN CRANE • JEYPORE GROUND GECKO
• INDOCHINESE BOX TURTLE • BUTTERFLY SPLITFIN •
YELLOW-SPOTTED TREE FROG • TENERIFE SPECKLED LIZARD
• RED-BELLY TOAD • VANCOUVER ISLAND MARMOT • NASSAU
GROUPER

I begin to plant a native prairie in our backyard. I bring my
children to a native plant nursery, where we pick out tickseed,
switchgrass, and big bluestem. I sign us up for a CSA and brain-
storm ways to minimize our use of cars. On weekends, we go to
local parks where my daughter gazes at tadpoles and my son digs
his hands in the sand.

All the while, I'm aware that parents have a psychological
need to believe they can keep their children safe, and that climate
change threatens that illusion.

I'm aware that the greatest reduction to a family's carbon foot-
print is to have fewer children.

I'm aware that I decided to have one child, but then had a
second.

I'm aware that there are no guarantees for my children.

PHILIPPINE EAGLE • NEW CALEDONIAN OWLET-NIGHTJAR
• GALAPAGOS PETREL • TRUE WEEVIL • GREAT INDIAN
BUSTARD • YELLOW GOLDFLAKE • PEACOCK TARANTULA •
DEVIL'S HOLE PUPFISH • MYANMAR SNUB-NOSED MONKEY
• BLACK CRESTED GIBBON • POLYNESIAN TREE SNAIL •
STELLATE STURGEON

In the late days of my pregnancy and the early days of my son's
life, I sometimes could not watch the news. I couldn't bear to see

what was happening. Or rather, what was happening had the power to make me lose hope. To stare at his small body—his belly button still weeping because the bit of tissue from the umbilical cord had not fully died—and feel so fully that our country was headed in the wrong direction. What was I to do? I nursed my infant. I ate bowls full of fruit. I took baths in herbs. I let my body heal. I lay down in the afternoon when others were around to watch my son. I went on walks outside. I carried him to the porch. I watched him squint in the sun. I opened the shades of our home. I snapped the edges of his cloth diapers. I pressed my forehead against the cool window of the door at night, when we were both awake, in need of something to drink.

SPENGLER'S FRESHWATER MUSSEL • WHITE-TIPPED GRASSHOPPER • SOUTHERN EVEN-FINGERED GECKO • ROSE'S MOUNTAIN TOADLET • RED CRESTED TREE RAT • RIVERINE RABBIT • SIBILLINI MOUNTAIN GRASSHOPPER • LITTLE GLAND FROG • WHITE-TIPPED GRASSHOPPER • GREEN SAWFISH • RED WOLF

It is despair. It is hope. It is a long O. An om. A prayer. A praising. Sometimes a pleading. Sometimes nothing at all but my steps moving forward. One day at a time. One waking at a time. One night at a time. Life, right now, with small children, when climate change looms large, and our country is not doing enough about it, is my hands open, asking. My hands on tree trunks. On babies' bodies. On grass. On laundry. On the washcloth as I wash bottles and the valves of my breast pump. On student papers. On this keyboard, now. My hands, reaching out, saying sorry, and please; saying can't we be tender? Compassionate? Can't we break through something with our elbows? Can't we heave our bodies against what is stopping us from changing our mindsets, our ideologies? Can't we get past these simple comforts? Can't we give up something so that they, in the future, will have something too? I know what fear is, and I know how hard it is to think about changing our lives, and I know we all feel small sometimes, and inconsequential, and maybe we are, but we are here. We are bodies on this earth.

NORTHERN HAIRY-NOSED WOMBAT • STRIPED GEKKO • EUROPEAN EEL • ORNATE GROUND SNAKE • GREEK RED DAMSEL • SPRING PYGMY SUNFISH • SOUTHERN BLUEFIN TUNA • GIANT CARP • PERUVIAN YELLOW-TAILED WOOLLY MONKEY • BACTRIAN CAMEL • SAPPHIRE-BELLIED HUMMINGBIRD • ADDAX

On a vast plains near the end of the Cretaceous period, a mother ceratopsian grazes with her child, lowering her frilled and horned head to the ferns and the cycads. The volcanoes have already been rumbling, spewing carbon dioxide into the air. The wind makes the grasses thrum and whistles through her spines. She tenses, alert, plucking thin leaves with her beak. What is it she's thinking? When she suddenly looks up and sees the meteors fall?

I lean my head against her flank and feel kinship.

BLONDE CAPUCHIN • CAVE GROUND-BEETLE • VIETNAMESE POND TURTLE • ESPANOLA GIANT TORTOISE • GIANT MOUNTAIN LOBELIA • SIERRA NEVADA BLUE • GREATER VIRGIN ISLANDS SKINK • WHITE LEMUROID RINGTAIL POSSUM • STAGHORN CORAL • SHENANDOAH SALAMANDER • WHOOPING CRANE • BLACK-FOOTED ALBATROSS • BICKNELL'S THRUSH • AMERICAN PIKA • HAWKSBILL

SEA TURTLE • RUSTY PATCHED BUMBLE BEE • MONARCH BUTTERFLY • SOCKEYE SALMON • RED-CROWNED ROOFED TURTLE

A species goes extinct. A civilization ends. Both are the uncomfortable if constant nature of life. And although I know I need to accept this—that everything dies, and humankind will eventually, too—the part of me that holds my children still needs to carve hope in the future. Hope in sacredness and responsibility and ecological kinship. Hope in bodies and community and connectedness and land.

BRAZILIAN MERGANSER • SUN STRIPE SHRIMP • CADDO CHIMNEY GRAYFISH • APPALACHIAN ELKTOE • ADELIE PENGUIN • CORPULENT HORNSNAIL • ATLANTIC RUBBER FROG • BLACK SOFTSHELL TURTLE • HOODED VULTURE • SLENDER-BILLED CURLEW • COMMON SKATE • SCIMITAR-HORNED ORYX • AFRICAN WILD ASS • SAHARA KILLIFISH • ATLANTIC HUMPBACK DOLPHIN • DAMA GAZELLE

In the backyard, cantaloupe sprout from our compost and I let them sprawl across the lawn. I breathe in air made of atoms that have circulated for eons, atoms also inhaled by crustaceans and brachiopods. I lower my head to the sweaty scalps of my children. Each of us animals on the eve of an extinction. Each of us alive to what we are becoming.

ADDITIONAL THOUGHTS
ON CONTROL

I do not know how to end this.

When I found out I was pregnant a second time, I lost control of my body. My body was rebelling, doing things I did not tell it to do. I set my hands to my abdomen and wondered what was happening. If my body was another's body, where was I?

Birth/Control.
Control/Birth.

Birth Control.
Control of Birth.

Controlled Body.
Body Controlled.

I've never been good at giving up control. Even with medication.

I once took Benadryl on an overnight train, hoping it would lead me to sleep.

I felt my body lighten. I felt my body ache for sleep. But each time my vision shifted, I fixated on the sensation and woke myself back up. My body and mind were a rubber band, stretched tight, and I was the aching tightness between them. I was tightened and tightened and tightened, until the sun started to come up on the horizon, and in the hazy dizziness of Benadryl and a lack of sleep, I realized I could not let go of myself. I could not turn my conscious self off.

My husband cannot control his body, either. For more than thirty years, his pancreas has failed to produce insulin. He injects himself instead, but even that sometimes fails, and his blood sugars skyrocket or unexplainably dip, leading to mood swings, dizziness, anger. When my husband's blood sugar is low, he'll eat anything in sight. When it's high, he'll pick fights I learn to ignore.

When I went to the yoga studio the weekend after the pregnancy test turned positive, I could not control my body. My stomach shuddered and a chill settled around me. I took deep breaths and reached for my toes, swaying in a hazy weakness. I was there and not there. I was in my body and hovering above. At the end of class, when we laid in Savasana, my chest caught—an upwelling of tears. I left the class shaking, no sense of who I was.

In those days, only yoga could return me to my body. I attended one evening class a week. And then two, and then three. I returned home to my daughter's face in her window. A glowing moon, awaiting my return.

Halfway through the pregnancy, I switched to a new class, with an instructor who proved fearless. She did not tell me to ease up, or that I shouldn't do certain poses. She did not hover three feet away with an uncertain eye.

Instead, she buttressed my body as I kicked into a headstand, and for the first time in my life, my shoulders supported me. Muscular arms and abdomen braced a taut, growing belly. I began to trust I wouldn't lose myself, or my life, with a second child.

It was a new kind of embodiment.

In the past few years, I have collected books by the Buddhist nun Pema Chödrön.

When Things Fall Apart.
Comfortable with Uncertainty.
The Wisdom of No Escape.

Reading them, it seems a kind of privilege: to have once thought I could stay grounded. To have thought I could plan a happy life.

My pregnancy was a daily trauma. The trauma of knowing that something was happening to me that I did not want to happen, and that I had nonetheless let it. That the time had passed to say no, and I did not say no.

God, grant me the serenity to accept the things I cannot change, the courage to change the things I can, and the wisdom to know the difference.

I remember sleeping under the stars one night at summer church camp. The heavens rotated above me, pressing my back into the earth, and I was just one body among many, infinitesimal and meaningless, humbled by stars.

Would the Buddhists say I should have accepted the pregnancy? That this was one of those things I could not control?

Have I spent the past three years fighting my attachments? My desires to control a future that I never could control?

When the time came, I woke in the night and paced through the kitchen and leaned into the kitchen counter and then the wall.

I knelt on the floor, flexing and unflexing my spine, and pressed my head into the bed's mattress. My body was burning, making the room disappear, and these were the breaths I returned to. This was the body I succumbed to. The ripping and blood and quivering and shaking. The small purple thumbprint left on the wall.

Birth uncontrolled.
Uncontrolled birth.

Birth requiring six
dissolvable stitches.

Afterward, my hip clicked for three months. My abdominal muscles, pushed apart during pregnancy, refused to come back together. When I laid on my back and lifted my head, a chasm formed around my belly button. A two-inch span of muscle-less flesh.

Afterward, I was floating on water. I was lost in a fog. I was a body receding to six millimeters behind my eyeballs. A body distilled into nothing at all.

Without telling anyone, I stopped at a tattoo parlor in town two hours before I picked up my kids from day care. It was and wasn't spontaneous, just like it was and wasn't grief.

In the parlor, the tattooist—a bald, soft-spoken man—talked about hometowns and migrations and his two broken marriages. He told me he could move anywhere he wanted and asked if I had kids. "I don't fit in a box," he said. "I make my own box. Are you surprised?"

His touch on my back was blessingly gentle. He asked me quietly if I was okay.

When I returned home that evening, with two children and a bandaged back, my husband crumbled near the oven, shocked that I'd changed my body without consulting him. "Why did you do it? Why am I not enough?"

From Louise Erdrich's *The Blue Jay's Dance*: "Conception is often something of a by-product of sex, a candle in a one-room studio, pure brute chance, a wonder. To make love with the desire for a child is to move the act out of its singularity, to make the need of the moment an eternal wish."

I sometimes wonder which experience of conception is best. Sex and conception as haphazard, a surprise, a woman accepting whatever comes, attuned to the miraculous mystery of her body.

Or sex and conception carefully planned, controlled, approached with pills, thermometers, and, if needed, injections.

Do we touch some throbbing mystery when we give up control of birth?

Or are all our ways of control inherently faulty, inherently flawed, prone to the 1 percent that will break expectations and leave us thrilled or depleted.

To reckon with / the slipperiness and instability of life / and emerge. / The machinery is in order / but we still / are fearful.

I regained control by reaching for words, for meaning. By reading books and writing essays, by teaching and planting seeds and seedlings in the garden. I took long walks and kept myself all too busy, and sat with trembling arms and trembling doubts and trembling uncertainties.

At yoga, I laid on my back, depleted. "Empty the contents of the pelvis," my yoga instructor said.

It took a long time for me to realize what I'd been taught to ignore. Most cultures have, at one point or another, practiced infanticide. Most cultures have, at one point or another, tended abortion-aiding herbs.

A few months before my son turned one, my husband scheduled a vasectomy. The surgery was a requirement we devised to save our marriage, but one day before the procedure, the urologist's office called to reschedule. An emergency had come up, and the doctor needed to postpone. When the receptionist suggested a new date the following week, my husband declined because he was too busy at work.

"I couldn't decline the birth just because it was inconvenient for me," I spat.

I remember turning away from my husband, my breasts leaking milk as my body constricted with anger. Men's bodies. Women's bodies. I wanted to believe it was the system that was faulty, but what if it wasn't? What made women's bodies so vulnerable to others' control?

In the urologist's office more than two months later, my husband sat in a reclining surgical chair, and I sat along the wall opposite him. For the first time, I watched my husband tremble while slipping off his underwear. One pale leg, shaking in the light.

This must be how it felt to watch me, I thought, and I imagined the reversal: all those times in the ob-gyn office, when I leaned back and opened my legs.

Thoughts are like time and feelings—fleeting. They pass. Notice them, but do not cling. You are not your thoughts, just as you are not your anger or joy or happiness or sadness.

After the vasectomy, my anger lessened. Like the slow unclenching of a jaw, it loosened and released until I could once again eat freely and no longer had to press a finger to the muscles beside my eyes. Something was over, and what followed offered, if not calmness, at least a respite.

A stone had been thrown into a pond. Cataclysmic ripples that then subsided.

It seems a strange system. We mourn the choices we did not make, and yet after enough time has passed, we forget there had ever been a choice to begin with.

The days pass and the days pass and the days pass.

I read books. I take walks. I plant seedlings in the garden.

I contemplate happiness.

I used to expect the "right" choices would lead to happiness. That if I were unhappy, it was because I had made some wrong turn and needed to recalculate.

Now I'm not so sure.

Maybe happiness is more ethereal. Not so much about choice, and more about presence. Am I here in this moment? Can I open myself to joy?

Or, if I had allowed myself to be present, would I have made different choices?

My son is two and a half years old. I drive him to the same day care he attended when he was just months old.

In those days, my son's face was a face I could not always mirror—he an infant needing someone to take care of him, and me the person yoked to take care of him—and I went through the routines and dropped him off and picked him up again later in the day, and sat with him at night when he awoke, hungry, and I did not let myself fully inhabit my body because I couldn't. Because a large part of me never wanted to be there.

I thought about leaving my husband, but didn't. I thought about leaving my children, but didn't.

Now things are easier, perhaps because my children need me less.

In the past few weeks, Georgia, Ohio, and Alabama have passed heartbeat bills and antiabortion laws that effectively ban and criminalize the procedure.

A woman can be prosecuted in Ohio if she leaves Ohio in order to have an abortion elsewhere. An eleven-year-old in Ohio was raped and is being forced to carry the child to term. Doctors in Alabama face up to ninety-nine years in prison for conducting abortions.

I once believed in the Bible. Now the whole book sits like snake-skin in my hands.

To be forced to carry a fetus to term…To not be allowed to make that choice…

I had an unintended pregnancy, and I love and came to love my son, but no, if I had another unintended pregnancy, I would not make those same decisions. I would not do that again.

From a book on feminism and self-care: "If you have a choice (and clearly, sometimes, whether it be for personal or professional reasons, you don't), reserve the right to say no."

From Sara Ahmed's *Living a Feminist Life*: "It can be rebellious not to be made happy by what should make you happy."

Also from Sara Ahmed: "We can mourn because we didn't even realize that we gave something up. The shape of a life can feel like a past tense; something we sense only after it has been acquired.

"But we might also know this: we can leave a life. It is not too late to leave a life."

What my husband and I laugh about most is our children. The way they harvest purple carrots in their underwear, both too young to be self-conscious. The way they yell at us from the backseat of the car, chanting in unison for ice cream or macaroni or bunk beds or pet chickens.

I watch them laugh and kick at each other, their soft bellies pressing against the straps of their car seats. They are alive with bodies of their own, and I am a body acquiescing.

I don't know how to end this. I don't know what to leave.

In yoga class, I learn that the hyoid bone is the only unarticulated bone in the body. The only bone that does not touch another.

I store this phrase in a notebook, as if it will teach me something about interconnection.

Bodies moving
against each other.

Bodies knowing when
and when not to let go.

In the backyard, a rabbit burrows under a yucca.

In the garden, a gnat bites the eyelid of my son.

Relax your hyoid bone, my yoga instructor says.

Relax what anchors the tongue.

CREDITS AND
ACKNOWLEDGMENTS

Just like children, books (and their writers) grow best in communities rather than in isolation. Many thanks to the editors of the following journals, which published earlier versions of some of these essays and offered valuable feedback and support:

About Place Journal: "On Race and Motherhood in America," May 2021.

Dark Mountain: "Animals on the Eve of Extinction," spring 2020.

DIAGRAM: "Message for the Animal Mother," spring 2022.

Ecotone: "A Cost Accounting of Birth," spring/summer 2021.

Literary Mama: "On the Silence of Regret," April 2018.

Michigan Quarterly Review: "On Contemplating a Second Child," winter 2019.

Museum of Americana: "On Breast Pumps and Bovines," summer 2019.

North American Review: "The Mother-Infant Dyad," spring 2022.

Orion: "BabyCenter: An Essay on Place," July/August 2016.

Prairie Schooner: "Birthwork in the Bible Belt," fall 2022.

The Rumpus: "A Political Pregnancy," January 2020.

Sycamore Review: "We Are Animals," winter/spring 2018.

In drafting, revising, and polishing these essays, I especially need to thank Scott Russell Sanders and the women in my 2016 Bread Loaf Orion Environmental Writers cohort, who bolstered

me and offered a much-needed community as I was just beginning this project.

I also cannot express my gratitude enough to Stacey Engels,
Sarah Chavez, Sandy Longhorn, Trisha Cowen, Marissa
Schwalm, and Lesley Bartlett, each of whom read drafts of
multiple essays and whose affirmation and encouragement—as
mothers and as nonmothers—did so much to reassure me that
what I was exploring was important and went beyond the self.

Thank you to Steffanie Mortis Stevens and everyone at Trinity
University Press for their support and belief in this book. I cannot
imagine the book landing with better people or a better press.

Thank you to all of the individuals named and/or alluded to in
this book, who shared their experiences with me, commiserated
and laughed, and/or offered companionship and care. Special
thanks to Sharon, Tracie, and Reesa for keeping me sane.

Thank you to Kevin, for going on the journey with me, and
for respecting and celebrating these essays even when I chose to
write about the most difficult parts.

Thank you to my children, who have taught and continue to
teach me so much. May this book not cause harm but, in some
small way, make the path easier for you and your generation.

Thank you to Adrienne Rich, Louise Erdrich, Carmen
Giménez Smith, Beth Ann Fennelly, Sandra Steingraber, and my
other literary foremothers, who in writing about motherhood in
authentic, nuanced ways gave me permission to do so myself.

Last, thank you to all of the women, men, and humans who
have reached out to me after reading one of these pieces to share
their own stories, struggles, and ambivalences about motherhood
or parenting. Listening to them and knowing that these essays
have resonated with others has been an honor and a deep joy.

**Jennifer Case** teaches creative writing at the University of Central Arkansas. She also serves as an assistant nonfiction editor at Terrain.org and is the supervising editor of *Arkana*. She is the author of *Sawbill*, and her work has appeared in *Orion*, the *Sycamore Review*, and *Fourth River*. She lives in Central Arkansas.